POST ROAD

SUBMISSION AND SUBSCRIPTION INFORMATION

Post Road publishes twice yearly and accepts submissions in all genres.

• POETRY: Editor, Post Road, P.O. Box 15161, Cincinnati, OH 45215

• FICTION: Editor, Post Road, P.O. Box 590663, Newton Center, MA 02459

• NONFICTION: Editor, Post Road, 203 Bedford Ave., Brooklyn, NY 11211

• ALL OTHER SUBMISSIONS should be addressed to the section editor and sent to:
853 Broadway, Suite 1516, Box 85 New York, NY 10003

*

Subscriptions: Individuals, $16/year; Institutions, $32/year;
outside the U.S. please add $6/year for postage.

website: www.webdelsol.com/Post_Road

ISBN: 0-9704430-1-3

POST ROAD

Criticism

Art

Nonfiction

Etcetera

This issue is devoted to those lost in the terrorist attacks of September 11, 2001.

Contributor Notes

Nelson Bakerman is a photographer and filmmaker. His photographs have been published and exhibited domestically and internationally, and are included in the permanent collections of the International Center for Photography, the Brooklyn Museum of Art, among other public and private collections. He was a member of Richard Avedon's Master Class, and is the former recipient of the Photographer of the Year award from both *Art Director Magazine* and *Philadelphia Magazine*.

Thomas Beller used to play the drums. Now he writes occasionally (*Seduction Theory*, Stories; *The Sleep-Over Artist*, Novel) and helps run a magazine (*Open City*) and a web-site (www.mrbellersneighborhood.com).

Edward Brunner has contributed material on Hart Crane, Weldon Kees, Melvin B. Tolson, and Harry Crosby, among others, to the MAPS website (www.english.uiuc.edu/maps/poets). With Cary Nelson, he is assembling a definitive edition of Crosby's writing and photography. A professor at Southern Illinois University (Carbondale), his most recent book is *Cold War Poetry* (University of Illinois Press, 2001).

Olisa Corcoran is a writer and photographer living in Durham, North Carolina. Her work has appeared in *The Carolina Quarterly*.

Rebecca Curtis recently completed an M.F.A. in fiction at Syracuse University. She is currently working on a collection of short fiction and teaching standardized test preparation courses. Her fiction has recently appeared or is forthcoming in *The Gettysburg Review, The Ohio Review, Noon, Fence,* and *McSweeney's*.

Brian Evenson is the author of five books of fiction, most recently *Contagion*. He is the Senior Editor for *Conjunctions* magazine and a fiction editor for *Denver Quarterly*. He teaches at University of Denver.

Myla Goldberg's novel *Bee Season* was named a New York Time Notable Book for 2000. She is currently working on a new novel concerning the 1918 influenza epidemic.

Although he lives and works in southwestern Wyoming, **Kevin Holdsworth** maintains a "rude and rustic hovel" in south-central Utah. He is a regular contributor to *Weber Studies, South Dakota Review* and *Junction*, and is currently co-editing an anthology of Wyoming poetry for Conundrum Press of Colorado.

Len Jenkinson was born and raised in the English Lake District and originally trained as a painter at the Chelsea School of Art. Married and a father to two grown sons, he's had a number of jobs in arts education but has since moved to full time writing—first poetry, then short stories—over the past five years. He has contributed to *London Magazine* and U.K magazines such as *English, Blade,* and *The Interpreters House*. He is currently looking to publish his collection, *Better Than Winning The Irish Sweep*. "I've always preferred American fiction to our British stuff. For years I've read Updike (which made me want to be a writer) and I love Rick Moody's work and of course Annie Proulx."

Jennifer Kronovet lives and teaches in New York City. She received an MFA in Creative Writing from Washington University in Saint Louis. Her poems have been published in *Poetry Northwest* and *Meridian*.

Ben Lerner is a poet living in Topeka Kansas.

Lee Martin is the author of a story collection, *The Least You Need to Know* (Sarabande Books 1996); a memoir, *From Our House* (Dutton 2000); and a novel, *Quakertown* (Dutton 2001). He is Associate Professor of English in the graduate creative writing program at The Ohio State University.

Cate Marvin's first book of poems won the 2000 Kathryn A. Morton Prize and will be published by Sarabande Books in August 2001. She has work forthcoming in *The Paris Review*.

Sarah Messer has received fellowships from the NEA and the Fine Arts Work Center in Provincetown. A book of poems, *Bandit Letters*, was recently published by New Issues. She lives in North Carolina.

Rick Moody was born in New York City. He attended Brown and Columbia universities. His first novel, *Garden State*, was the winner of the 1991 Editor's Choice Award from the Pushcart Press and was published in 1992. *The Ice Storm* was published in May 1994 by Little, Brown & Co. Foreign editions have been published in the United Kingdom, Taiwan, Germany, Brazil, France, Italy, Spain, Israel, Japan, Holland, Portugal, the Czech Republic, Poland, and elsewhere. (A film version, directed by Ang Lee, has recently been released.) A collection of short fiction, *The Ring of Brightest Angels Around Heaven* was also published by Little, Brown in August 1995. The title story was the winner of the 1994 Aga Khan Award from *The Paris Review*. Moody's third novel, *Purple America*, was published in April 1997. Foreign editions have been published or are forthcoming in Portugal, Brazil, France, Germany, Italy, Holland, and the United Kingdom. An anthology, edited with Darcey Steinke, *Joyful Noise: The New Testament Revisited*, appeared in November 1997. In 1998, Moody received the Addison Metcalf Award from the American Academy of Arts and Letters. In 2000, he received a Guggenheim fellowship. His most recent work is a collection of stories, *Demonology*, recently published by Little, Brown & Co. He has taught at the State University of New York at Purchase, the Bennington Writing Seminars, the Fine Arts Work Center in Provincetown, and the New School for Social Research. He lives on Fishers Island, New York.

Kate Moos is the Poetry Editor of *The Ruminator Review*. She received her M.F.A from the Bennington Writing Seminar. She lives in Saint Paul, MN.

Chris Offutt is the author of two books of short stories, *Out of the Woods* and *Kentucky Straight*. He has also published a novel, *The Good Brother*, and a memoir, *The Same River Twice*. His writing has received many honors, including a Whiting Award, a Guggenheim fellowship, and an award from the American Academy of Arts and Letters.

Steve Orlen's new book, *This Particular Eternity*, was published by Ausable Press in 2001. He teaches at the University of Arizona and in the low-residency MFA Program at Warren Wilson College.

Robert Pinsky's most recent book of poetry is *Jersey Rain*. He is also co-editor of *Americans' Favorite Poems: The Favorite Poem Project Anthology*.

Liam Rector's books of poems are *American Prodigal* and *The Sorrow of Architecture*. He directs the Writing Seminars at Bennington College and he lives in the Boston area.

Frederick Reiken is the author of two novels, *The Odd Sea* and most recently *The Lost Legends of New Jersey*. He teaches at Emerson College's graduate program in writing and lives in western Massachusetts.

Scott Seward lives in Philadelphia with the love of his life, Maria Danielson. He is proud to write about music for *The Village Voice*. He has never read anything by Greil Marcus, but he'll get around to it someday. Ask him about the time that he wrote liner notes for The Best of Foghat CD. You can e-mail him at skotrok@earthlink.net.

Michael Snediker has no real problem with Uma Thurman. His poetry has been published in *The 12th Street Review*, and will most likely appear elsewhere soon.

Jason Wilson has written for *Conde Nast Traveler, National Geographic Traveler, Salon.com, Travel & Leisure, Saveur,* and the *North American Review,* among other publications (including some he'd rather not admit to, such as airline in-flight magazines). He is the series editor of *The Best American Travel Writing.* ❖

FICTION

POST ROAD

The Sweater, The Pair of Shoes, and the Jacket

Rebecca Curtis

A daughter disobeyed, and the mother of the daughter hit the daughter very quickly with her hand, a thing she had not done before in the past. Soon the daughter disobeyed again, and again the mother struck the daughter in the face with her hand and then also with an object that had been nearby. The daughter cried and ran away but soon came back and disobeyed, and the mother took the object that had been placed nearby for use and broke it upon her daughter, who moved from the room on her knees and came back and was beat by the mother who had become three mothers with three objects that had all been nearby, and the daughter on her belly moved very slowly from the room and eventually came back and disobeyed, and the mother took the daughter's head in her mothers' hands and pulled it close to her own and held it in that place for hours, and now that the mother had given the girl a sweater, a pair of shoes, and a jacket, one item upon each departure, the girl was dressed. ✧

Vegetable on the Hoof

Chris Offutt

I was one of those people that everyone knew would eventually stop drinking, and the whole town was grateful that nobody died in the process. I drank for the full-body buzz, and whisky only—rot gut, rye, bourbon, blend—if it was brown, I drank it down. This is perfectly acceptable in a college town, but I am 42 years old. Two years ago I gave up drinking. It is my hope that strangers will think I am a cool older guy and not another burnout drifting the streets. The fashionable look here is hat-hair and a backpack.

This isn't about me, it's about Jim—a man of the people, a thrift shop dresser, a poet who wouldn't kill a cricket. All this stood Jim in good stead thirty years ago, but street cool does not age gracefully. Time slides on down the road. Hair falls out, plugs the drain, fills the brush, and has the nerve to turn gray.

Jim got by on part-time jobs, which is important for a poet who proudly pooh-poohs an academic career. He deplored the author photos with hair carefully brushed to look as if it hadn't been carefully brushed. Most of all, he despised the readings during which the anecdotal introduction to the poem was both longer and more interesting than the poem itself. In his youth, he published a single poem that was included in a number of important anthologies. The poem was a villanelle, an old form currently out of favor. You could say Jim was a villanellist.

His wife Mary is gorgeous, bipolar, and a socialist. She didn't believe in property, and that extended to what people did with their own bodies, more particularly what Jim did with his wiener. Her medication made her grow a seasonal beard, but when she went off the meds, she could drink until the cows came home. She was easy to get along with and never wore makeup. People liked her. Jim loved her. They kept it together through the ancient recipe of cheap rent, no kids, crap jobs, and luck.

Jim slept with a lot of women in town. If it was your girlfriend or wife, you didn't mind all that much, because it was just Jim, Forgivable Jim—the hippie poet with loose britches. In many cases he was performing a community service by helping rocky marriages through a tough patch. Women knew they could turn to him for a casual affair. Jim was warm, discrete, and relaxed.

According to national magazines, a small college town offers the highest quality of life if you don't mind fraternity boys date-raping sorority girls on the weekend. Student bars are clustered downtown in convenient walking distance to campus and the county jail. The manufacture of fake IDs is a thriving business. Scattered along the edges are the grown-up bars full of lonely people who like to get pickled together. For years I was one.

The first time I walked in a bar sober, the sheer volume of cigarette smoke was overwhelming. Everybody shouted to be heard above the jukebox, but it didn't matter because they were all talking at the same time anyhow. No one listened. It wasn't so much that everyone was drunk except me, but more like I was peaking on acid and they were all straight. The light was crooked, the eyes were glassy, and the mouths were moving with no sound. Laughter came from elsewhere, like word balloons on the margin of a comic strip, and I could read their thoughts and they were all thinking the same thing—drink, sex, sleep.

Anyhow, Jim was a mess and he called me and I owed him because he stayed loyal when I went off whisky. I met him at the bar where I hit the water hard. I told the bartender to keep it coming. People bought Jim shots, which he kept "in the well," meaning on reserve for later, and when the amount surpassed ten, Jim began giving drinks away. Folks took this as a terrible portent. Rumors flowed like silt through the tavern, and most prominent was the worst—his wife had finally gone ahead and found her own lover. After all, Mary hadn't been around lately. Jim was plenty morose, but after a few drinks he swore me to secrecy. He swore everyone to secrecy. Pretty soon the entire bar knew about it, and no one talked about it, like the first grade teacher who's a kleptomaniac, but her husband goes around once a week and squares everything with the shopkeepers. Forgivable Jim, hometown Casanova, was no longer able to get it up.

The whole bar mourned Jim's impotence. Folks would have worn black, but no one wanted the place to develop the reputation as a pretentious arty joint, where everybody scribbled intently in ratty notebooks, chain-smoking at the table for hours, costing waitrons entire months of rent money in lost tips.

As word got around about Jim's problem, an endless variety of cures cropped up, and he gave them all a whirl. For a week he wore ladies' underwear. He ate snails, caviar, and ginseng. He went to a strip club on the interstate, a porn shop on the county line, and a hypnotist in the next town over. He went off milk. He gave up meat and took up wheat. He tried acupuncture, creative imaging, and sleeping in a hammock. He sat on his hand until it fell asleep, then masturbated, and sure enough he claimed it did feel like someone else, but to no avail. Nothing worked, and all over town marriages were suffering.

Jim's impotence made us close. He talked and talked, confiding in a way that is more associated with women than men. I was surprised to learn that he was working on a seventh manuscript of poetry. After his auspicious debut, he was so afraid of rejection that he never sent a poem out. He wished he'd traveled more. He always wanted kids, but the time had never been right, and now there was no time. He'd frittered, puttered, and dawdled.

Into the bar came Mary with no beard, meaning no medication, and Jim left immediately, as if they were drinking in shifts. She sat at the end of the bar and sipped vodka, utterly lovely with lustrous hair and swimmer's shoulders. I joined her with a double water on the rocks. She's missing a tooth on one side and makes no effort to hide it, a dark little gap that perfects her beauty.

People in the bar made a big circle around Mary like she was the center of a crater where the giant meteor hit that wiped out the dinosaurs, and getting near the edge would invite death. It is a sad fact that when a man has sexual problems, people blame the woman, and nobody wanted to get near Mary in case it was contagious. An even sadder fact is that women used to run things in the old days because they are so smart, but men were stronger and meaner and took the world away from the women. It still works that way, too—brawn beats brains every day. Look at the newspapers and look at the Senate, and look at the fate of small-time dictators as opposed to big-time thinkers.

Mary finally began talking about the Butler Bull Farm where Jim worked three days a week. Cattle ranching had gotten so competitive that farmers will Gomerize a calf, a surgical procedure that reverses the penis so that all its functions occurred the opposite way, spraying backward between its legs. After it matures, the farmer periodically released the Gomered bull into a pen full of heifers. It mounted the ones that were in heat without the risk of pregnancy, thereby informing the farmer which heifer to artificially inseminate. Mary said the vet who invented the procedure was named Gomer and had made a fortune. She said that cattle farming has reached the point where cows were no more than vegetable on the hoof.

If you were a man, you just crossed your legs and winced, thinking that a Gomered guy would have to sit down to urinate, which is a terrible blow to masculinity. If you were a woman, you began thinking of all the trouble you'd save by having a Gomered man handy—no more fear you might be pregnant, no more guilt of abortions, no more dropping out of college to have a baby, no more abandoned dreams slowly congealing to hatred of men, which you transferred to your children. Your daughters became strippers, and your sons were so psychically Gomered that they will later take it out on women in a terrible Gomerian cycle.

I sat in the bar and drank more water, wishing it was whisky but sticking to my guns. Smoke and chatter clogged the air. I sensed someone close behind me and spun on the barstool, but no one was there, and I tried to act like I was just waving to a woman across the room. She gave me an odd look, but I continued to wave, and she undoubtedly decided that I'd fried my brain with too much acid.

I heard that LSD of the 1970s was cut with strychnine, which stayed in your body, lodging along the spine. Drinking enough water would flush it out. For years I feared a full-blown acid flashback—the materialization of a hydra while I was on the interstate, causing my car to flip into the median, bounce ass over tea kettle and skid to a stop with the metal top peeled back like a sardine can, cassette tapes scattered in the grass, the spinning tires slowly winding down, and my severed limbs bleeding out due to youthful experimentation with LSD. This fear at least kept me driving slow. The reality is, acid flashbacks happen all the time. They are no more than quick motion on the periphery, like a startled animal leaping to cover. I have reached the point in life where I welcome a gentle flashback—but not tonight while Mary was talking.

I have to admit that the Gomer business made me feel funny. I look at Mary and guzzle water like it is going out of style—which is true considering how bad it tastes from the faucet. Junk music floated from the jukebox. Harvesting bull semen for future use was not an easy proposition, and I realized that Mary had been talking for quite some time. Bulls weigh an average of 1200 pounds, are bad eating, and won't work. They aren't good for much except fertilizing a cow. Prime bull semen is worth more than gold and cheaper to store, but getting it is tough. The female enters heat, the male enters the female, and the sperm enters the egg at a thousand miles an hour. If all goes well, the transaction is quicker than a double play. If not, the farmers have wasted money and there's a frustrated bull with a three-foot pizzle.

Mary explained that in the interest of economics, farmers now use a phony cow. Steel plates are welded to an iron frame and draped with a cowhide heavily dosed in pheromones. Inside is a sleeve to accommodate the pizzle, and at the end of the sleeve is a receptacle to collect the semen. The fake cow rolls on wheels down a chute to a lonely bull. The typical bull is not a gentle creature. A fragment of his puny brain knows that this particular cow isn't quite right, and the bull will often beat the daylights out of the metal frame. The faux cow rocks and rattles in an alarming fashion. Inside the cow's giant hollow ass is a man wearing gloves who helps the bull ejaculate. That job pays well, and that man is Jim.

Ever since, Jim had been unable to fulfill his marital duties. Mary began weeping, the tears glistening in rivulets down her cheeks. I quickly suggested that Jim quit the job. Mary laughed through her tears, a rainbow in mist, and said that he's left sixty part-time jobs for the noble reason of poetry, but now he refuses to quit for the ignoble reason of sex. I nodded. I said I understood. I really didn't in the least.

It was the first night in a long time I felt a real strong desire for whisky. Usually it's just a faint urge, like a rubber band shot from a distance striking bare skin, but her story pushed me across the line to a full-blown craving. Rows of shiny bottles beckoned with their promise of instant heat that would shoot from my throat to the heels of my feet, followed by a cheery smile and the anticipation of a great night laughing with wonderful people. Whisky is social grease and I'm a lonely person who just wants people to like him. I reminded myself of waking up thirsty and sick, as if a pipe full of woe ran from my head to my guts. The car was somewhere, and I was somewhere else, and the remorse was lying right there between the sheets. I narrowed my vision to eliminate the amber gleam of beer glasses moving through the tavern like fireflies at dusk. I chugged water like it was going out of style, which in fact it is.

Mary had asked for help. I was flattered and told her it would be a downright honor to extricate her husband from a fake cow's ass. She was effusive with her thanks before she left. A smoky saloon full of people watched her depart with a bouncy saunter, like a door-to-door salesman on his way to the car for the final paperwork to close a big sale. Those bums should stay at home, and the damn phone salespeople are the worst. I have learned that politely telling them my number is for a business phone will make them delete you from their computerized list.

According to great thinkers, when troubled, you are supposed to find your answer with God or nature, or both. After a tiring but inspiring walk of solace along the muddy bank of the nearest river, held firm by stacks of junked cars to prevent erosion, an idea made me call a veterinarian and lie like a rug. I told him I needed to transport a prize bull cross-country, along with some heifers that are in heat, and was there a drug to make the bull easier to handle. He said yes, then put me on hold. Eventually the vet told me where to get the pizzle dope.

Late that night I parked a mile away from the Butler's Bull Farm and crossed a fence carrying triple the vet's recommended dosage, a drug called Phenyltetracylamite that is actually cut with strychnine. I snuck into the barn and dumped it into the bull's food bin, which was conveniently available and clearly marked. Then I drove home to bed.

On Monday night the bar got the liberal-going-to-seed gang. This town is full of old hippies, and someone should tell them they don't look cool anymore, they just look old and fat. The sight of bald men with ponytails means that twenty years from now we'll see grey mohawks on guys with potbellies and combat boots.

About ten o'clock, I go to the bar, where Mary and Jim are together for the first time in months. They moved through the crowd like royalty, dispensing waves, nods, hugs, handshakes, and kisses. The general mood rose as if each regular drinker was the petal of a flower opening to light. Mary glowed and Jim was confident. Part of their bodies touched the other at all times, like a massage therapist who's moving around the table and wants to maintain continuity. It was wonderful to behold. Word spread rapidly and the bar filled because it was a time to be jubilant, a new deal of celebration—Jim was back and no wife was safe. Yee-haw!

I felt for the first time in many years a glimmering pride of accomplishment. I'd restored order to the community by helping a friend. I toasted myself with water, grateful for it. I could feel strychnine loosening throughout my body. ✧

White Square

Brian Evenson

The black square on the table is meant to represent Gahern's estranged wife; it is presented as such at Gahern's request. The gray square beside it stands in for the black square's new husband, also presented as such at Gahern's request. Though Hauser has offered him the full gamut of shapes and colors, Gahern insists upon remaining unrepresented. Nothing stands in for him. When Hauser suggests to Gahern that the investigation might proceed more smoothly were a shape allowed to stand in for him as well, Gahern simply refuses to reply. *Perhaps a green rhombus?* suggests Hauser. Gahern asks to be returned to his cell.

The investigation, Hauser repeatedly reminds himself, is progressing poorly. Gahern will only speak when both the black square and the gray square are on the table before him. Even then he says little, if anything, of use. When questioned concerning the whereabouts of the gray and black squares, Gahern says nothing. He will not indicate whether these squares represent persons alive or dead. *These are meant to stand in for them, they are symbols,* is all he will indicate, gesturing to the squares. When Hauser hides the squares in his lap and asks Gahern where they have gone, Gahern only says, *They are in your lap.*

Such are the facts as Hauser has recorded them:
—Individuals represented by gray and black squares both disappeared, 12 October. Said individuals absent three months now.
—Said disappearance preceded by Gahern's own sudden disappearance, 17 August. When, 8 November, Gahern reappeared and returned to former workplace to request reinstatement, he cited his reason for being absent as *continued persecution by his estranged wife and her new husband.* Said persecution, he indicated to lathe foreman, had concluded, was not to be resumed.
—After Christmas, Gahern found to be living in black and gray squares' residence (Gahern's former residence before estrangement from black square), with both squares having disappeared. This last fact compelled Hauser, at Commissioner Torver's request, to open an investigation.
The additional information Hauser has amassed through interrogating Gahern is marginal at best. Hauser's investigation, Gahern insists, is a

form of persecution somehow perpetrated by black and gray squares from a distance—their persecution of him has unexpectedly resumed. He is certain they will never leave him alone. He fled to escape them, came back only when he had taken steps to assure an escape. Now, he can see, he escaped nothing.

"What steps did you take to assure an escape?" asks Hauser.

"It is of the utmost importance," claims Gahern, "that I be provided a new identity and be allowed to leave the city immediately."

"Of course," says Hauser. "We will assign you a new identity: Rhombus, Green. Just answer a few questions first."

In Gahern's private world, Hauser thinks as he sits in stocking feet, a cup of hot water before him, *there is only one shape. Square.* There are, however, two colors. Or rather two shades—gray and black. Each of which admittedly might be described as a lightening or darkening of the other.

Through the window, through square panes of glass, he can see down into the central courtyard. The courtyard consists of eight rectangular slabs of concrete, of a slightly lighter gray than the gray square meant to represent the new husband. Beyond, he can see the even façade of the north wing of Branner B. Gahern's office is in the south wing of Branner B, a building designed by one Edouard Branner if a plaque on one marble corner of the building is to be believed. In his travels about the city, from crime scene to crime scene, Gahern keeps an eye open for Branner A, the precursor of Branner B. He has never seen it. Perhaps Branner A was torn down to make way for another building, perhaps even for Branner B. Whatever the crime that presents itself to him, Hauser's first question is always the name of the residence or residences attached to the crime.

Yet this crime is different. There is no crime scene to visit. He cannot ask his habitual question. Instead, it is just he and Gahern, in a narrow room, a table between. Only words. Or as now, just he himself, in his office, alone. Only thoughts.

One shape, he thinks. *Two shades.*

Why is it that Gahern will not take a shape and color to represent himself? Can I force him to accept a shape and color?

Was it prudent, wonders Hauser, *to have allowed this manipulation of shape and shade to commence?*

"Shall we try again, Mr. Gahern?" says Hauser. "Where you were during the month of October?"

"Fleeing the persecution of the following," says Gahern, reaching out to finger first the black square then the gray square.

"Of what did said persecution consist?"

"They constantly disturbed me," says Gahern. "They appropriated my residence, interrupted my sleep, impeded me on my path to work, insulted me, interfered with my operations on the lathe in my place of employ—"

"—Yet, Mr. Gahern, curiously enough, I have a sheet of paper before me that claims that the reverse of what you say is true. On seven separate occasions, complaints were filed against you by your ex-wife and her new husband, the last culminating in a restraining order."

"This, too, is part and parcel of their persecution of me."

"Where are they, Mr. Gahern? What have you done with them?"

"These are meant to stand in for them," says Gahern, gesturing to the squares.

"I'm afraid that doesn't answer my question," says Hauser.

Gahern folds his arms, tightens his lips.

Hauser receives a telephone call. It is Commissioner Torver. *How is the investigation?* Torver wants to know.

"It seems to have become a sort of geometry problem," says Hauser.

"Yes," says Torver, "so I hear. Or a child's game. Do you think it wise, Hauser? Shall I step in so we can have a word?"

Hauser assents and recradles the headpiece, awaits Torver's arrival. As he waits, he looks at the square panes of glass in the window. *Surely,* he thinks, *I will be reprimanded.*

He realigns the already aligned piles of paper on his desk, picks up the gray and black squares. *If Torver were a square,* he is starting to wonder as Torver enters, *What color square would he be?*

Yet, he suspects in looking at the man's face, in watching his lips move, that a square would not be the proper shape for Torver.

Hauser has two days and then the investigation will be taken from him, Torver seems to be saying. The gist of his words comes to Hauser as if from a distance. *Like Gahern,* thinks Hauser, fingering the squares, *I myself prefer to remain unrepresented.* Apparently Hauser's methods are most unorthodox, but Torver is willing to let him extend said unorthodox methods for a short period. Hauser must not let him down. *Perhaps a rectangle,* Hauser thinks of Torver, but soon discards this in favor of a simple oval. By the time he has settled on a dirty white for the color, the simple oval has finished its admonitions and is just walking out, leaving Hauser alone to wonder what the Commissioner's shape and shade signify.

*

Perhaps, thinks Hauser, *I could produce a series of squares, moving in almost indiscernible increments from black to gray, and substitute them consecutively for each square on the table.* After a number of careful substitutions, the black square would wither to gray, and the gray square would ripen to black. Gahern might realize something was happening but perhaps would not understand what. Suddenly he would perceive that the square he thought gray was black, and the square he thought black gray.

And what, Hauser wonders, regarding his reflection in a pane of glass, *would be the point of that?*

Anything could happen, one of them suggests, either him or his reflection, perhaps both.

But nothing significant ever does.

Something could.

You have two days. You haven't time to experiment.

Perhaps, one of them thinks, *both squares could be gradually changed until they are nothing but two pieces of slick white cardstock, squares of light shining up from the tabletop.*

He closes his notebook, turns each square face down. Time has passed. He has learned nothing. Gahern is still there, just on the other side of the table. Unrepresented, still himself. *I, too,* Hauser insists, *remain unrepresented.* He holds his hand before his face, assures himself it is still a hand.

He watches the hand remove a cigarette from a pack, extend it toward Gahern.

Cigarette? he hears his mouth offer. He knows that the voice he hears in his head sounds different to him than it must sound to Gahern, listening outside the head that speaks. Who is to say who hears the voice correctly?

Gahern takes the cigarette, tucks it into his breast pocket. "You look tired," he says.

"What do you know about Branner A?" asks Hauser.

"Who?"

"Not who," says Hauser. "What. And A, not B."

"I don't know anything," says Gahern. "I don't even know what you're talking about."

"Look," says Hauser. "Let's forget everything. I don't care what you did with the squares. I'm willing to forget all that. Just tell me where to find Branner A."

Gahern does not answer. Instead, he regards his fingernails. To Hauser, from the other side of the table, the fingernails appear to be normal. There is no reason that he can see for anyone to be looking at them. Yet he cannot stop looking at them.

Hauser's time all but gone, his methods failed, he has let Torver down or is about to. *A final effort,* his reflection tells him, *gird yourself.*

He brings in a piece of paper, blank, places it on the table between the black and gray squares. He sits across the table from Gahern, watching him.

He lets nearly an hour slip by without speaking. He looks at Gahern's face, trying to will it into a simpler shape.

He takes a pencil from his pocket, draws a short line on the paper. Carefully he tears up first the gray square and then the black square.

"Care to add anything?" asks Hauser.

"You're guessing," says Gahern.

"Am I?" asks Hauser and, standing up, leaves Gahern alone in the room. He leaves behind the scraps of squares, the pencil, the paper.

Outside, he takes a place looking through the mirrored wall. Next to him are four people whom he chooses to represent in the following fashion: oval, triangle, rhombus, triangle. Through the mirrored wall, he watches Gahern sit at the table, head in his hands. He seems, for once, shaken. Hauser goes to fetch a cup of hot water; when he comes back, nothing has changed.

"Now what?" asks one of the shapes beside him.

Oval. Red, Hauser thinks, perhaps orange. He holds one hand before his face to assure himself it is still a hand, then shrugs. "Wait," he says. "Nothing to do but wait."

He watches through the glass. Having sipped away his water, he goes in search of another cup.

When he comes back, he finds Gahern has pulled his chair about to bring his back to the mirrored wall. He has taken up the pencil, is hunched over the paper, his arm moving furiously. Hauser wishes he could see Gahern's face.

Gahern remains hunched over for some time. At last he puts down the pencil, brings both hands together before his body to do something with the paper. Hauser finishes his water but does not go back for more.

When finished, Gahern pulls his chair back to its usual place at the table. He has folded the sheet of paper into a white box, a simple cube. The pieces of the squares are nowhere to be seen.

Once Gahern has been returned to his cell, Hauser enters, sits alone with the box. He examines it, draws a picture of it in his notebook. It is the sort of box that children make, and having made them himself as a child, he knows which seam he must unfold first. He knows what to do.

He turns the seam, and the box cracks open. Inside are the scraps of the black and gray squares. Dumping them out onto the tabletop, he forms a little heap. He unfolds the next seam, then the next, until the box lies flat on the table, nothing but a creased piece of paper.

There is nothing written on the paper. Indeed, all that remains of Hauser's original mark is a thinness in the paper where Gahern has fastidiously rubbed said mark away.

An hour later, Hauser is still staring at the blank sheet of paper, at the pile of scraps. Perhaps it is a denial, perhaps a confession, but in either case, he is no closer to understanding anything. There is no point, he knows from past experience, in asking Gahern to explain further.

He looks at his watch. He begins to piece the squares back together, the black one representing—he can still bother himself to recall fleetingly—the wife, the gray one representing her new husband.

Soon the investigation will be taken from him. He will pass along the evidence—the fragments of squares, the folded sheet of paper—and then he will tender his resignation to a dirty white oval. Leaving Brenner B for good, leaving the unrepresented Gahern, he will walk into the street and lose himself in the crowd among shapes of all kinds. Until then, there is nothing to do but wait. ✧

The Museum of Speed

Len Jenkinson

Wilson is building a snowman with his son. First, they roll a snowball 'round the garden 'till it's big enough to make the body. But the big ball leaves a track where you can see flattened grass; by the time they've made a smaller ball for the head nearly all the thick snow on the terrace is rolled up. Wilson can see Jackie doesn't like this — he doesn't like it himself; they'd both pictured a snowman in the garden *as it was,* standing on the perfect snow curving down under the hedges. Even when its face is done with bits and pieces from the house it seems more like they've destroyed something than made something. Still, it's got Jackie out of the house—that was the idea, to get him out of the house and let Celia explain tomorrow's funeral arrangements to her mother. She's been here at her mother's for three days now, but Wilson's just driven over. He'd been struggling on the farm all week, getting in late to cook and check the lad had everything ready for school next day.

Back inside with Jackie on the floor in front of the TV the talk 'round the table is all about money and shares, and about Cliff's cars. There are twelve of them altogether, including the two Jags, the Allard and the Fraser Nash and the Daimler SP250. There are models of them all 'round them now, most of them scratch-built by Cliff right down to the engraving on their little copper nameplates. A toolmaker by trade, Cliff had taken the only risk of his life in '69 and spent what his father left him on buying up the old fish depot on the quay and two old Jaguars. This '30s-style house was his own, a gift from his father-in-law for all the work he'd done for him, and for ten years he'd drawn plans and done bookkeeping for people in the evenings and worked all day every day building the car museum up. It was in all the guidebooks now and advertised all over, and for the last ten years, with the remodelling of the quay and doubling of tourism in the town, it had made him a very comfortable living.

Celia suggested they get a bottle of whisky down. There were at least a dozen of them up there; firms gave them to Cliff at Christmas, but he never drank more than a glass of ginger wine on Boxing Day. He'd been a very sober man, an exceptionally reserved man with an odd resemblance to Donald Pleasance. And now, at 53, he was dead. Suddenly. Found slumped at his lathe in the place he liked best, in his workshop behind the museum in this south coast holiday town.

"Mum, wasn't there a letter or something you wanted Wilson to see — about some catalogues or something?"

Celia's mother gets up and unlocks Cliff's rolltop desk. Before she shuts it he gets a glimpse of its ordered contents — one compartment completely filled by Cliff's neat stack of Benson and Hedges cigarettes. Like his wife his mother-in-law is tall, but monochrome and angular without Celia's ample covering. As well as the cards there are now eight or nine letters on the table. He doesn't read them but scans the print under the letterheads of motor and engineering forms. There's one from Classic Car magazine, talking of Cliff's 'Unique and encyclopaedic knowledge of pre-war marques,' but Celia passes him a handwritten one, on blue paper. It's from a Mr. Lance Talbot. Mr. Talbot doesn't seem to know Cliff is dead. He'd enjoyed talking with him on the Brighton concourse in May, but could he possibly let him have the promised leaflets featuring early Mulliner Park Ward specials?

"I'll have to write and inform him about Cliff," his mother-in-law is saying. "But if you could go down sometime Wilson and see if you can find what he's after—Cliff seems to have promised him something."

'Round the table the whisky is beginning to take effect; despite the sadness he feels a sense of occasion—the liberating effect of change. And there is the snow. Beyond the thick velvet curtains it has started to snow again. "I can go down there tonight and have a look if you like, Helen."

"Oh there's no hurry Wilson." She is drawing the curtains, shutting out the ravaged garden. "It looks very bleak out there to me. It's snowing heavily again now."

"Actually, I feel like a walk out, if you let me have ... his keys, I can go down through the woods and then 'round by the prom."

'Actually' he is thinking about going for a *real* drink. He's had a hard week, and the whisky has given him the taste for it.

And then, there's Becky. On the way back he could call in at Becky's.

Outside with the door shut behind him everything sounds muffled and his feet make that 'crump' sound on the snow. He goes up the steps between Cliff's ornamental lamps and out the side gate. Out on the road a Bentley glides by leaving its shiny white tyre tracks printed in the snow. Way below he can see the ropes of coloured lightbulbs 'round the harbour. The town was built on the wooded hills 'round the harbour, but the heart has been ripped out of it by a bunch of property developers. It's only up here you get a flavour of how things used to be — the resort for the better off — the big villas among the trees with their chimneys and gables, their high stone walls lining the pavements. He takes the road past the tiered flats and architect magazine bungalows cantilevered out over the hill. The wood is roaring. Way below between the trees the surf along the beach road is white just like the snow. Funny how this snow had come but Cliff hadn't seen it — he'd liked snow; Wilson remembers a Christmas with snowflakes out the window, Cliff drinking his ginger wine, tinkering with the tree lights, explaining the difference between wiring in parallel and series. Not that he would have seen these woods in the snow; he wasn't a man to wander about in the snow — he wouldn't have seen the point. But he was no less for that, with his torque wrenches and his gauges. Wilson misses him more than he'd thought — feels a sense of loss he hadn't thought. Cliff wouldn't have *seen* these woods in the snow, or the white surf, but it's just ... Suddenly the wind drops and he stops to light a cigarette ... it's just — they're *here*. They're here and Cliff isn't anymore. The mystery of that.

It wasn't that he'd been close to Cliff; he hadn't even got on well with him. They'd had nothing in common. He remembers the first time Cliff came to the farm, he couldn't understand why there was so much mud — so much shit — the untidiness of the place. Then the van coming to take the bullocks away — it seemed to embarrass him. He was too gentle for the place — too *organized* to cope with it. He'd been such a *private* man, all those years just quietly going through the routines of his life — he hadn't *asked* to be born after all; he'd just found himself in the world: and now he'd left it. There was something *'unbidden'* about it all — like the snow had come. Unbidden.

Coming down the path above the promenade he can see the big *MOTORAMA* sign over the roof of the coach depot. Cliff always called it 'The Museum,' but everyone knows it as Motorama. Opening the door the familiar smell of oil and clean metal hits him, the strip light motors herald the familiar walls — dark blue to chest height like a bus station, the green lino with drip trays under each of the cars. He still can't understand how Cliff got their tyres so clean; did he paint them black? Through the back, everything, including the tool racks, is labelled with red Dymotape. The files in the cabinet under C for coachwork are all in alphabetical order and he soon finds the '40s specials — those beautiful flowing lines — but closing the drawer turning to go he gets a fright. Cliff's boiler suit on a hanger on the door *still holds his shape:* through long use it holds the sagging essence of him.

It was here in the pub he'd first met Becky. She was working behind the bar, serving her marine or her mercenary or whatever he was. Ordering his beer now he wonders why it is women's other blokes are always called 'Nick'. This one was working as a scaffolder and wore the extra tan belt slung round his jeans like a gun belt; the effect was completed by a red checked shirt. He still has a clear picture of him. His eyes were the colour of raisins, perfectly round shiny raisins. Nasty. Celia had introduced Becky as an old school friend, and Becky had suggested they call 'round sometimes — just 'round the corner her flat was. They had called 'round. But then he'd started calling on his own.

The pub doesn't change. It still has the loud patterned carpet and fruit machines flashing by the door. In summer it's full of holidaymakers, but in winter the locals come back in — not the rich ones with their poodles and Bentleys you see at the deli and the patisserie down the street but the men who live alone in the flats 'round about. For some reason a lot of them are ex-military. He can hear a couple of them now 'round the corner, talking out of sight.

"As far as I'm concerned Rex they're what they've always been." The voice grows quieter. "Bloody terrorists."

"And that Mandela —"

"Biggest bloody terrorist of the lot — I'd go back there tomorrow if things were what they were."

"It isn't working now, is it?"

"Of course it isn't, and it isn't *going* to bloody well work, *and I'll tell you why it isn't.*" The voice goes even quieter. "Because they're not capable of government. They're not equal and they never *will* be equal, and that's all there is to it. Anybody who's been out there will tell you the same." The voice drops to a triumphant whisper. "Most of the bastards can't even clean themselves properly."

It's a big bar and the staff have put a couple of Calor gas heaters in the middle of the patterned carpet. He gets himself a whisky and pulls a chair over to one of them. He's thinking about Cliff again — something he once said about the blacks. He'd only heard Cliff offer an opinion on an 'issue' twice, once on cruelty to animals and the other time on the blacks; he said he'd noticed we were keen enough to have them on our Olympic teams.

She had other callers too, Becky. One of them was the manager of the Westminster Bank up the street — he'd spotted her on the beach and started to call 'round. He nods to a big man he'd spoken to one afternoon in here, a driving instructor. When he'd said he was a farmer the man had talked about guns, said he was in a gun club. She didn't talk about her other visitors much — except early on she'd said something about Nick. She said he'd shot one of Celia's old school friends, over in Belfast it was.

He'll have another big one then make a move — he mustn't be too late back. The trouble is, the more he drinks the more he thinks about the farm. He ought to be working on the accounts now; the laptop is still in the Land Rover. His father took a dim view of his being over here for longer than the funeral, but he'd said he could be getting on with the accounts. They were in a real mess *last* year, but this year! They're hopeless. Surely his father and Fletcher can manage the farm for three days. They won't open the mail, they'll leave it for him. It's no handicap for Fletcher to stay on the bloody farm; you can't prize him off it — he'll be in the barn now scraping and repainting some piece of machinery ready for spring.

Fletcher would have made a much better son-in-law for Cliff.

When Becky opens the door to him it happens all over again: that emptiness, that giddiness. She is so slim, so insubstantial: what he sees is not her but the style of her dress — not her hair but a hair*style*. Her face is a picture: kissing her he remembers how the first time he did it her teeth got in the way — real hard things that surprised him.

Her kid coming onto the landing is the same: an elf. An elf who never speaks.

In the kitchen they sit at the little Formica-topped table by the window, the big window he saw lit up as he came along the road. There are no curtains; the snow beyond the big gate pillars glows orange from the streetlight.

"I'm over for the funeral."

"Yes, I heard." She is putting on mascara, pulling a face that distorts her voice. "He canth haff been vey old, was he?"

"Only fifty-three."

Her mascara is in a scruffy plastic case with a cracked mirror, she lets it clatter down beside a plate with eggshell and cigarette ends on it. "How's Celia taking it, is she very upset?"

"She's ok. She's been too busy organizing everything — I expect it'll hit her when she gets home."

"I suppose she was quite close to him wasn't she — being an only child." She lights a cigarette, balances it on the plate, then tilts her head to brush out one side of her hair. Her hair is dark brown and perfectly straight. "How's the farm?"

He lights a cigarette himself and looks out the window. "It's getting worse. I'm supposed to be doing the accounts ... Fletcher's all for telling the old man how bad things are, but I don't think he understands himself really. Silly bugger's still as happy as a pig in shit most of the time ... except we haven't got the pigs anymore ... It's just not big enough. Nothing less than 1200 acres makes enough anymore."

She makes some coffee, and they go through into the big room where the TV is always on. In a few minutes she will send the kid off to his computer games and they will make love on the settee. Following her, she is so slim, a hanger for her clothes. When she came to the farm, Celia, who has a good figure, looked big beside her — suddenly more real. And Celia *talked* so much more. Sitting across from her now, her knees form the base of a spreading V; the space between her thighs is a void, an emptiness he wants to loose himself in. *She doesn't talk because she hasn't got anything to say;* what they will do in a few minutes will be largely meaningless to her. Sex with Celia isn't meaningless, and afterwards they talk about the farm. But the farm is FINISHED. On paper — on the screen, it doesn't add up anymore. What they do every day — bringing in the cows, milking them, making the silage, has no point anymore; it's just a ritual.

He can feel the cold coming off the black windowpanes behind him. It was hot that summer she came to the farm; when he brought her back in the Land Rover, they went outside into the garden down there — what she called 'the meadow.' It was all overgrown, stretching down to the old house on the bottom road. There were a few poppies and flags left from the garden the house had before it was split into flats but it was mostly weeds, willow herb, and long grasses. They'd make a kind of nest down at the bottom against the hedge — she was wearing a cream dress with wild roses on ... But then they'd found the gap in the hedge and gone through to discover the old potting shed the men were using. There were armchairs in there and an empty brandy bottle, and on the wall a big Union Jack with photos of men in uniforms. In the middle they'd put that picture, of a black man being lynched. The poor bastard had shit himself. That was when she'd told him about Nick, how he'd sometimes come up through the meadow at night and climb in her window. And how he'd given her the gun.

He knows where it is. He looked at it a long time ago. It's in the cobwebbed cupboard under the basin, wrapped in a cloth. He should have left ages ago, but after they'd made love she'd found a bottle of cheap brandy and they'd had another go, on the floor. *Jesus, she was wild tonight.* He's in the bathroom now, washing the smell of her off him. But there's no towel, only a pair of transparent orange panties over the bath tap. Christ! How can she live like this; half the time there aren't even any fucking lightbulbs — toilet paper — in the cupboard, maybe there's a new roll, but bending down he feels dizzy and a bit sick. It's still here. Behind the mug and the soap dishes in its grey cloth. And he watches himself — feels himself — picking it up, slipping the heavy lump of it into his Barbour on the door.

But then he sees the wind.

This is the clifftop road — he must have taken the long way 'round; even though he was so late, Celia will think he's got drunk somewhere worrying about the farm, but he's way past that. *Everything is so white and silent* ... he can't work it out: who has made these tracks, what has shaped the snow like this? Curving down under the hedge then away and 'round like competing ski tracks untwisting into this great patterned plain.... rising to the thing itself. It's like something from Cliff's streamlining display — 'The Silver Wraith' — or the *'Speed of The Wind'* — not snow but the wind *showing itself* in snow: the wind made visible. While he's been in Becky's the wind has been about its business. Elemental. Light years beyond that filth in the potting shed, regardless of Cliff's death — regardless of the farm being bankrupt — the wind has been about its business. And he has never seen anything so *unearthly*.

And as he looks he feels a kind of lightness, a *joy* as the weight of his worry falls away. He takes the heavy lump of the gun from his pocket and hurls it far out over the cliff edge. He's not that badly off — in the scale of things. He still has a great deal. Perhaps he and Celia could take on the museum, Helen would like that — Cliff would like it — *Cliff wants it* — take it on but expand it. Not just cars but something bigger — THE MUSE-UM OF SPEED; speed in the air and on water — the speed of animals even, and birds — the speed of winds and waves. He imagines the displays — a graphic chart comparing speeds — 'From Glaciers To The Speed Of Light,' blow up photos of what the wind does to deserts and clouds, photos of river bores and tornadoes and diving birds and aeroplanes' wings.

Maybe Fletcher and his father could take over the old ice plant—the bit Cliff never used—put a clear PVC roof on it and get some old tractors and farm machinery in. If nothing else, it would keep them happy.

He wants to get back now. He must get back to Celia. But as he leaves he sees the thing is changing, losing its sharpness — losing its shape. A plume of snow is blowing off the top. When he last looks, it has almost dis-appeared. ✧

The Iowa Review

WINTER 2001-02

DEAN YOUNG,
CHRISTINE HUME,
DANIEL WEISSBORT,
MEG MULLINS, GREGORY
SPATZ, JOELLE BIELE,
ALBERT GOLDBARTH,
LAWRENCE REVARD,
DEBORAH KEENAN,
AND A FEATURE
ON PORTUGUESE
WRITERS.

308 English Philosophy Building, Iowa City, IA 52242
www.uiowa.edu/~iareview

POETRY

POST ROAD

A History of Kansas

Jennifer Kronovet

Her plumb line led her
to the center of the country. Sleep
was the weight and the rope.
Sleep, the livid logic of it, beaded
across the land like mercury.
Motel beds. Sleeper cars.
Her head against the window.
Each night's bioluminescence.

The signs were there: every hill was a slow
breath, the sky was the catafalque of night.
As she entered, her condensation
on the window fogged fields into clouds.
Here would be the rest of roots in winter,
the flat sleep of grass under snow.

As she stepped off the train, night was torn
like any other. Soda machines. Kitchen light. Cough.
There would always be this state
and the state people dreamed about.

Scenic Overlook

Jennifer Kronovet

There were places only we could ruin—
exposed sky, scree placing each foot
into falling. The joking lurch of a ledge:
a worm in the night-box of thinking.

Getting lost we blushed into the day,
redder and redder into perhaps we will never turn,
turn here towards the swimming height
of a view. There are clues to how you learned

to speak in how you touch me. There are places
only we could leave: cows followed their shadows
on the hills. I followed one with my eyes
as you recounted the number of times

one saint's body was unearthed and moved
by tapping on my back. How can that be holy
I asked? Think of mosaics, you said, which I
no longer walk over without injuring the dead.

From The Lichtenberg Figures

Ben Lerner

II.

Pleasure is a profoundly negative experience, my father
was fond of saying under water. His body was carried
out like a wish. We paid out last respects as rent.
The mere possibility of apology allows me to express
my favorite wreck as a relation between stairs
and stars. I take that back. To sum up, up

beyond the lamp's sweep, where a drip installed by heat
still drips—some tender timbers. At thirteen, I had a series
of dreams I can't remember, although I'm sure
that they involved a rape. I'm brutal because I'm naked,
not because I'm named, a distinction
that the scientific and scholarly communities,
if not the wider public, should be expected to maintain.
No additional media available (but isn't it beautiful when a toddler
    manages to find and strike a match.)

V.

I confused her shadow for an accent.
I confused her body for a simplified prose version of *Paradise Lost.*
I confused her heritage for a false bottom box.
I confused her weeping for expressed written consent. 'Choked
    with leaves'

is the kind of thing a child would say in this rhomboid fun park and yet
you've been saying it under your breath, way under, ever since
the posse of stars rolled in. Obese with echo, Milton tips his brim.

Twenty-one years of destroying all evidence of use has produced
    extensive evidence of wear.
So I hike up my graphite trousers and set out
for an epicenter of great beauty and peacefulness. 'A major event.'
She called the publication of a portable version 'a major event.'
She called my adjusting the clasp 'a major event.'

She confused my powerful smell for a cry from the street.
She confused exhalation for better living through chemistry.

Why Sleep

Cate Marvin

I might miss something. The man who paces
his dog as my eyes walk with him between the slats
of blinds. The neighbor girl who always wakes
me anyhow with her cry, *You're such an asshole!*

And I've been inclined to agree since I heard
him tell her one four a.m. he hoped she'd die.
I might miss the nice blue and red flashing the cop's
car makes on the blind, as it hums outside—

as I strain to make out this low murmur, *But she locked
me out, Sir.* And I would not get to see the lovely
orange that will take this place down—and it will,
eventually, with all the gas pouring from my stove's

unlit pilot—Lovely, lovely flames! I want to watch
them consume us—and then I'd still be awake, standing
out on the chilly street, having saved myself, and having
saved myself I'd have to watch everything but me

go down. And don't I care for the neighbor girl?
Maybe I'd save her. I thought of taking a cake,
or some tea, down there tonight. But I was too afraid
she'd come to her door with an array of bruises
I'd have to address. Sleep? Those bruises are hers,
not mine. I lie, I lie. Here, inside the beat, deaf even
to the beat, only able to be the beat: muscle, muscle,
heart, thighs. When the cop car goes away, he stays.

And then there's another sort of cry. In the morning,
I rise ringy eyed—and I suppose I rummage
through nights like a raccoon, too, having to sort

out the rotten from the rotten. This night's food satisfies;

day's a porridge that will suffice. And what's there
to say in that plain light, when I see him out walking
the dog? Hello, hello—sorry about the disturbance
last night. *I must have slept through it,* I lie.

Ocean is a Word in This Poem

Cate Marvin

One centimeter on the map represents one kilometer on the ground.
River I can cover with a finger, but it's not the water I resent. Ocean—
even the word thinks itself huge, and only because of what it meant.
I remember its lip on a road that ran along the coast of Portsmouth.

Waves tested a concrete brim where people stood to see how far
the water went. Sky was huge, but I didn't mind why. The sea
was too choppy and gray, a soup thick with salt and distance. Look,
sails are white as wedding dresses, but their cut is much cleaner.

No, I never planned to have a honeymoon by water, knew it'd tempt
me to leave your company, drop in. Ocean may allow boats to ride
its surface, but its word cannot anchor the white slip of this paper.
It cannot swallow the poem. Turbulence is on the wall. The map—

I would tear it, forget how I learned land's edge exists. I would sink
into the depth of past tense, more treacherous than the murk into
which our vessel went. Now when I pull down the map, eat its image
and paper, I'll swallow what wedding meant. Salt crusts my lips.

Rabid Dog

Sarah Messer

After she had swallowed him
completely (taste of soap-chalk,
ammonia, her mouth smelling
like water, like a dog's mouth),
she forgot the vows and how
she got there—the stranger's
kohl eyes leading her
to the broom closet and his hands
festooned with rings.

After all, her husband was a stray dog—
in the yard he carried a mirror
on his back, his eyes flowering.
He spent his days in the city
snapping at bees, getting his nose stung.
In the evening, he returned
with a mouth full of fur.

Sundays, she watched him
in the garden swallowing sticks,
his own arms, dragging
his rear legs like a wedding gown.
To him, daffodils were now
a bouquet of knives. He snarled,
shook his head, left, right, an impatient
bride, tried to see himself
in the mirror on his back
like the bride reaching behind herself
for the last button.

Finally, at a cocktail
party, he politely leaned over
and bit the wrist of a neighbor.

She passed a tray of canapés, saying
"The best thing to do is take him
out behind the barn and shoot him!"
A tinkling of laughter, then doom.
Her bangs flipping back like tidal waves.

Truth is: she had been his wife
two hours when she selected
a new lover—what was his name?
(In the cramped dark fumbling,
smell of chlorine, an entire forest
of brooms falling.) When they were
through, a bare bulb exposed
the tiny room: he wore a beard, and
in the janitor's sink he washed
his hands over and over again
like a raccoon.

Looking at Satan

Sarah Messer

Since his fall, Satan hasn't known who he is anymore. Simple truths have become hidden. Kissing women, he thinks: will they taste like fruit or meat? When he kisses men, their lips feel like bread crust, their skin like unwashed sheets. For my sisters, screwing high school boys in the boathouse became a habit. They enjoyed the deviance, their skin that smelled like mildew and lifejackets. If Satan was actually here on earth, he would certainly not be my poor father, retreating after the fact to walled cities, selling painted roosters as luck charms in golf resorts. He would certainly not be the man at the party who grabbed my hand saying softly, "This is difficult, but someone ought to tell you: in the past few months, you've gained a lot of weight." Looking at Satan, you can find no landing ground on his face; his left eye rolls towards the west wall, his nose slides into his cheek. He would certainly be a man, though; hairy, the way that flies can be hairy, with tight iridescent skin like the flies that infect horses with bots. Death-defyingly handsome. And sickening. Appearing perhaps in the form of a long lost uncle. So beautiful that my sisters would collect the soda cans he slurped and the spoons he licked and make them into altars. They would shun the boathouse boys and practice kissing each other. So beautiful that my brothers would ground their speedboats on marshes, zoom their motorbikes off trails. At night they would dream of bending over backwards and falling into him like a pool, and wake up sweating. Even my father would devise transparent ways of keeping Satan up late in the parlor trying to grasp his mutable yet irresistible countenance. Only my mother would know the truth and not be fooled. Unfortunately, she would have had such a rich history of useless homilies that when she spoke the truth about Satan, no one would listen. Years later, when her rantings actually came from the voice of an old woman, she would finally be heard to say: "The devil's in this house, and he is using us to remind him of himself." Then she would take all the mirrors down and bury them in the back field.

In A Certain Place, At A Certain Time

Kate Moos

Dread thrills her, and then relief,
as, waking in a mildew of stale gin
sweated out during the apostrophized night
of shallow sleep, she realizes how little

damage she's done. Her house is not on fire.
She hears the saurian busses rumble on time,
dieseling at the corner. Only she is badly
broken, swollen, petulant with remorse.

She wonders what she has done. And she
has done nothing, she remembers
as imperfect recollection sets in.
She has done nothing at all.

Only spent a life in a room that blinks
with blue light, talking to the television,
convinced that this is what is possible.
Another cigarette, another drink.

The Prince

Kate Moos

It is not impossible to live with a heart half-dead, the dauphin
in exile learns, minding its mild murmur in the middle
of the starry night, from the upstairs window surveying

his demesne anonymously. He would be king!
Call fools to his knees, tear his own hairless flesh,
get at that itch, and have for breakfast what he wished.

But the purplish valve can only curtsy.
We get used to it, he thinks,
thanks to our genetic bearing and regal reserve, good

as any Connecticut matron's. He imagines the crown's
heft, its weight on his brow, and imagines killing
the rabble, no quarter for the bovine lumps who

know him not in his rags, them and their gap-toothed
daughters. For them there will be no choking
on mercy, no goddam heart, no flower.

THEATRE

POST ROAD

Responsibility, Justice, and Honesty: Rehearsing Edward Bond's SAVED

Ken Rus Schmoll

Saved by Edward Bond was produced by Theatre for a New Audience in New York City, and opened on February 25, 2001. The production was directed by Robert Woodruff, and Ken Rus Schmoll was the assistant director.

I.

Midway through the rehearsal process of *Saved*, I went with my friend Sam to see the film *A Time for Drunken Horses* by Kurdish director Bahman Ghobadi. The film depicts Kurds living in the mountains between Iran and Iraq, focusing on a family of young children whose parents have died. The eldest son, still an adolescent, becomes the head of the household. With his siblings, he must figure out a way to raise money to help their deathly ill brother. Though a work of fiction, it is stated in the film by the director that it is an honest representation of life for the Kurds.

The title refers to the climactic sequence in which a convoy of people feed their horses vodka in order to keep them warm as they trek over the mountains into Iraq. In the convoy is our young protagonist, with his brother strapped to a horse. Halfway up the mountain, they are ambushed by soldiers guarding the border. Everyone must flee off the road and down the steep mountain face. However, since the horses are in fact drunk, they collapse. Because of his brother, our hero can neither leave nor get the horse to stand.

I had such a bewildering and intense reaction to the film. Nothing in the film was remotely recognizable to me. The landscape, the language, the way of life—no electricity, no running water—and most especially the problems these young Kurds faced were completely foreign. My experience of watching it was disorienting, since I could not see myself in it at all. I felt trapped but also compelled to reexamine both the familiarity of my own life and the alien world of the film.

My experience with the film stemmed from my work on *Saved*. Because of the play's foreignness, investigating it required a depth of effort I had never before experienced. I was primed to not dismiss *A Time for Drunken Horses*. I was ready to make a constant and unrelenting effort towards it, in spite of the challenge it presented.

2.

It was a few hours before the first press preview. The cast had performed Saved before an audience for a week so far, while continuing to rehearse during the day. The next three performances would include the press. In two days, the play would officially open.

Woodruff had gathered the cast for a final company talk. He reminded them that they are "responsible for giving voice to a class of people that isn't normally given voice to in the theater, in the commercial theater especially, and it is a great voice, a very poetic voice." He reminded them to work for honesty and integrity in each moment of the play. He reiterated Edward Bond's instruction that they cannot "take a night off," or "do matinees." Bond had told them that they were "responsible for making each performance a personal search for justice."

Notions of responsibility, justice and honesty are not typically called upon so resolutely and unabashedly for the performing of a play. And yet these notions had seeded the rehearsal process from the beginning and helped the production grow into what dramaturg Kathleen Dimmick called a "successful working confrontation" of several great artists.

3.

Edward Bond was born into the working class in 1935 in north London. *Saved* was his second play to be produced. In 1965, it was the last play to be banned by the British government under strict censorship laws. Since then, he has written more than fifty plays, adaptations, translations, and television plays as well as volumes of essays and published letters. His writings are all deeply political. To Bond, the act of making theater is always a political act.

Robert Woodruff is renowned in this country for his controversial stagings of classic texts (including *The Duchess of Malfi* at A.C.T. and *Richard II* at A.R.T.), his collaborations with the Flying Karamozov Brother's (including *The Comedy of Errors* at Lincoln Center), and as original productions of several Sam Shepherd plays. Admittedly, he has burned many bridges in the regional theater world. "Several theaters will never have me back," he says. Since theaters often rely heavily on their subscription and box office revenues, they feel the risk of producing controversial work is too great. He is a purist in his art, in that he won't settle for a comfortable interpretation of a play. He will expose the darkest underbelly of a play because he is interested in the theater's deepest potential as a catalyst for societal and personal change.

Jeffrey Horowitz, Artistic Director of Theatre for a New Audience, is committed to presenting bold, intelligent productions of classic plays. He had produced Woodruff's apocalyptic version of Middleton's *The Changeling* in 1997 and since had been eager to collaborate with Woodruff again. Horowitz said, "When we came up with *Saved*, Robert was hesitant at first. He thought that he was too old to direct it, but I thought it was material that he could really inhabit."

Horowitz knew Bond would have to be included in the collaboration, and so eight months before rehearsals began, he and Woodruff visited Bond in England. The three men spent an afternoon together. "Basically, Edward talked," Horowitz said. "He was very intense and very brilliant. In answering our questions, he would riff and just go for a long time, moving seamlessly from politics to philosophy, from sociology to theater." Neither American apparently said much at all. Bond agreed to let them produce Saved.

Later, at a meeting with voice teacher Cicely Berry, Berry asked Woodruff why he wanted to do the play. He replied, "I don't know." Horowitz remembers thinking, "If there was ever a play you had to know why you were doing it, it was *Saved*." He asked Woodruff if there was at least an area of exploration in the play that interested him. Woodruff said yes, and on that shaky ground they proceeded. "I knew he could do a great job," Horowitz said, "even though Robert didn't. My trust and respect for his work were a positive influence on him in our collaboration."

4.

Saved is about a group of working-class people. It follows the story of a family (mother, father, and daughter), a strange young man who lives with them, the daughter's new boyfriend, and a gang of friends. The thirteen scenes jump erratically forward through time, depicting the frustrations and tensions of living in their world. While some of the scenes convey moments of both lightness and tedium, others contain shocking portrayals of violence and neglect.

In an essay entitled *On Violence*, Bond writes, "The cause and solution of the problems of human violence lie not in our instincts but in our social relationships. Violence is not an instinct we must forever repress because it threatens civilized social relationships; we are violent because we have not yet made those relationships civilized...Violence is not a function of human nature but of human societies."

5.

As dramaturg, Kathleen Dimmick provided Woodruff with piles of research. "He said, 'Just bring me everything,'" Dimmick says. Areas of inquiry spanned the history of juvenile social forms in post–WWII England, contemporary youth culture, childhood and the imagination, how philosophical ideas can prevent or encourage human development, literary criticism, and, of course, Bond's letters and essays.

Sources included E. Ellis Cashmore's *No Future: Youth and Society*, William Finnegan's *Cold New World*, Freidoune Sahebjam's *The Stoning of Soraya M.*, Douglas Milburn's *Filicide*, and *the Mythic Reality of Childhood*, and Philip Larkin's *Collected Poems.*

From Woodruff's letter to the cast before rehearsals began (accompanied by a thick packet of this dramaturgical research): "It will be important that our exploration includes a kind of situational analysis that Edward often speaks about as well as work on a rich emotional life. It is the kind of inside/outside approach to performance which comes from understanding: what it is that is being portrayed as well as its full bloodied portrayal."

6.

Woodruff told his designers that he didn't want to get caught in a time period. He said, "I wanted something that spanned forty years, that wasn't locked in a moment, that you couldn't nail down in terms of a moment, because in a way, the play is a 20th century play that's more alive in the 21st century."

The main component of Doug Stein's set design was a cinder block wall. After structural engineers were brought in to guarantee that the stage of the American Place Theater could hold its weight, it was built by Polish masons. It was L-shaped, and with a hanging gray curtain, a large three-sided box was formed as the main playing space for the scenes.

The wall was real. It had integrity since it was built like walls in the real world. Between the wall and the curtain, however, there was a gap that exposed a section of the back wall of the theater. It disallowed the illusion that we were someplace else. We were in a theater, and there was indeed a wall.

"Nothing we do anywhere in the piece can be theatricalized, nothing can be dishonest," lighting designer David Weiner remembered Woodruff telling him. "Everything has to be honest. We can't dress anything up." He wondered, how do you make lighting interesting and honest?

One day, Weiner was focusing a steep light that would hit actors standing against the wall but will not hit the wall itself. He had not moved it into place yet, and at that moment, it was casting a huge angular shadow on the wall. Woodruff arrived at the theater and seeing the shadow, said, "Cool." Weiner said, "We can't do that, Robert. It's not honest." Woodruff smiled. Weiner understood that doing anything to the wall with light—texturing it, coloring it, casting shadow across it—would begin to erase the wall's own integrity.

Originally, Weiner and Woodruff thought about using practical lights like standing lamps and fixtures. They thought that exposing the source of the light was more honest than hiding it. They were removed, however, since they began to create the illusion of an actual house onstage, with outlets and plugs, and for this production illusions were not truthful.

The decision was also made not to paint or distress the look of the wall.

At a certain point during previews, someone noticed a dark smear on one of the steel doors built into the wall. It had developed over time from the hair gel used by one of the actors during a scene in which he leaned against the door for a long time. Should it be washed away? Stein said no, indicating that the stain was now a part of the history of that door.

With costume designer Kathy Zuber, Woodruff again wanted no evocation of a discernable time period to emerge. He said, "It was a hard thing, because then you didn't really have a visual reference. While it wanted to be poor, it didn't want to be about just poverty, because it was something more than that. There was a different kind of poverty that we were talking about; there was a poverty of culture, of opportunity, not so much always about material poverty, but it was about a poverty of possibility."

Zuber collected matronly schoolmarm dresses, striped polyester wraparound dresses, leather jackets, fur-collared coats, cuffed jeans. It was a collage of the second half of the 20th century. The design was grounded in today, but it also hearkened back to various years in the past. This allowed the audience to enter a play written in the '60's as well as see how it resonates in our current society.

7.

Woodruff asked composer Doug Wieselman to write music for the scene changes. The decision was made to expose them with bright light. The audience watched as members of the running crew, dressed in street clothes, executed the transitions, often involving rather extensive furniture moving. Wieselman said, "Robert suggested I try integrating the textures on the stage with the music. He also wanted the music to move the play along but not to comment on the action of the play."

Wieselman got large chunks of broken cinder block from Stein, and began to explore the possibilities of what sounds they could produce. He said he took the recordings and "slowed them down, processed them through the computer, looped them." Some of it sounded like a scratchy record that skips, while other sections sounded like someone dragging heavy bricks in circles on a paved road. He said, "When the sound was still not full enough, that's when I started adding guitar."

Early in the process, Wieselman said he veered away from these recordings. "I started composing all sorts of other stuff that was all wrong, like dark organ sounds. One piece sounded like a spaghetti western. In the end, Robert steered me back to those cinder blocks, which all along I knew I would somehow get back to. I don't know why I did that. I guess sometimes you have to go far afield in order to see the right direction."

8.

"It's really not hard to find actors who want to connect with something passionately," said Woodruff. "They want to feel a real relationship to material that transcends what they normally feel. An actor, by nature has to be able to invest in whatever they make but to also feel the greater sense of purpose, social identification, and just understanding the brilliance of something. That's the art."

That greater sense of purpose was felt more strongly when Edward Bond himself flew from his home in Cambridge to attend a week's worth of rehearsals. His presence, as Dimmick pointed out, "introduced American actors to the seriousness of an enterprise, which is not always common in our theater practice."

Edward Bond is a living legend. The day before he arrived, members of the cast jokingly pleaded with Woodruff to not start the next rehearsal with one of their scenes. Actress Randy Danson had heard of his reputation for being "quite scary." Woodruff commented that, with very few exceptions, he had lately only been directing the work of old, dead playwrights. What would it be like to have Bond in the room?

The next morning there was a slight tension in the air as Bond and his wife Elizabeth were introduced. Woodruff announced, "Let's take it from the top." And then realizing that he never uses that phrase, he muttered only half out loud, "I'm already speaking differently."

By the end of the day, however, the tensions were gone. At the end of Bond's stay, Danson confided to Elizabeth, "It's so funny how we were all so terrified of his coming, and now we don't want him to leave." Elizabeth replied, "Oh no, he loves Robert. If he hadn't liked what was going on the first day, he wouldn't have come back."

9.

During scene six, a baby is killed onstage. The audience doesn't see the baby. It sees the black carriage in which the baby is lying medicated. The attack is perpetrated by a gang of young men, whose unspeakable actions include punching it and ultimately stoning it to death. During rehearsals, the question pervaded: How do five 20-something actors believably enact this vicious scene? It is the scene that Woodruff assumed would be the most difficult to investigate.

Bond conducted an exercise one afternoon. First, he placed a cup in the center of the room and asked, "What is it?" Someone said, "It's a cup." And Bond said, "It's a bus." There was a decided silence. Bond then asked again, 'What is it?" Someone said, "The sun." And Bond said, "It's the sun? And you're that close to it?"

Bond was asking them to invest an object with qualities that weren't its own and to do so truthfully. Of course, this task was impossible, but during the exercise, he repeatedly asked them, "Are you telling the truth?" To say that the cup is the sun was obviously not telling the truth, but by not even reacting to its potential heat and brightness was an indication that their own imaginative responses were not yet real for them. What was needed was greater effort, a constant and unrelenting effort.

By the end of the exercise, the actors were handling the empty baby carriage as if it held a baby. As the actors threw stones, they vocalized as they worked, told by Bond to give voice to their pain. Though the exercise was cryptic, in the end, it was clear that the actors had reached a threshold with the scene. When they're stoning the baby, they're, in effect, trying to kill their own pain.

Woodruff said, "Edward led them to it, but he didn't state it. It was very Stanislavky. I always knew it had to be personal, but Edward found the door that, collectively, they could investigate personally. Largely due to his intervention, I think ultimately that scene was not as difficult as a lot of others."

10.

Scene six provided a technical challenge as well. What should be put in the carriage to create the sound of punching a baby? Of a stone hitting a baby? Leah Gelpe, sound designer, tried a series of objects: raw bread dough, bedding, a sandbag, a cabbage, modeling clay, a cabbage wrapped in modeling clay, a cabbage wrapped in duct tape, a cantaloupe, a pile of sliced deli meat, and raw chicken.

Questions arose: does it sound too hollow? Is it too wet? Is there enough "slap"? Is it loud enough? At times, everyone stood in the rehearsal room, heads cocked, listening intently as Leah threw rocks in at the various objects. There was never a consensus. Of course, no one knew what the sound of stoning a baby actually was, but somehow everyone knew what it didn't sound like.

During tech rehearsals and the first few previews, a raw chicken was used. It was tied into the carriage, covered in plastic, and surrounded by a fireproof blanket. "Eventually," Gelpe remembered, "it began to sound hollow, like a basketball. So I spent an hour one morning in a supermarket on 125th Street, surreptitiously punching item after item in the vegetable, fruit, and meat sections. In the end, I selected a smoked pork shoulder."

If it was struck too hard with the fist, the resulting "thud" was too dense and heavy. If, at the last second, the fist opened slightly and relaxed, the correct "slap" from the back of the fingers was achieved. Some of the actors needed a lesson in punching the pork shoulder.

11.

During scene four, the newborn baby cries continuously from offstage. The characters onstage perform domestic activities like watching TV, eating dinner, and getting dressed and hardly take note of the baby at all. The stage directions indicate a series of precise sounds made by the baby: "The baby screams with rage," "The baby chokes," "The baby whimpers pitifully," "The baby cries much louder." Bond reinforced the importance of achieving this score as a counterpoint to the onstage scene.

The first time in rehearsal that Gelpe brought in a recording of the baby crying, the effect was palpable when she played it under the scene. Each of the actors, in turn, burst into torrents of uncontrolled laughter, as did everyone else in the room. It was extremely uncomfortable, and everyone realized the profundity of this scene that on the surface seemed so simple. The cast wondered how they would be able to rehearse the scene without going crazy. In fact, Edward Bond recalled that it was this scene that drew the harshest reactions from critics and audiences when it was originally produced.

Norbert Butz, one of the actors and a father of two young children himself, commented that the baby sounded perhaps too old. It was already able to produce specific consonants and syllables. The baby needed to be a newborn, and Gelpe ultimately recorded four different babies before finding the right one.

12.

Robert Woodruff: "It was very easy to identify with the macro social, political voice of the play. To me, the hardest thing was finding the identification with the micro vision of the play. Finding the personal vision, Edward's personal vision, the details of this life, the family, this society, and then where I connected with it. It's always easy to wear your politics kind of exposed, but really the activation of your politics requires a certain kind of empathy and investigation, which you really have to put yourself on the line for, as opposed to just buying into some liberal catechism of thought. Ultimately, you really have to take it very personally in order to make something that resonates in a personal way, beyond just a kind of generic political statement of how tough it is to be in the underclass. And I think that was always the ongoing challenge, confronting the material and making the play."

13.

Edward Bond is a man in his 60s, but he has the questioning mind of a child. It was remarkable how he was able to open up moments in the play as if he had never seen them before. One day, he asked an actor, "Why do you say, 'O'? You could have said, 'Eh,' but you don't. Why is that?" The actor was forced to stop and reexamine this most minute issue. Later, Bond suggested to him, "I think the 'O' is more desolate, isn't it. I think 'Eh' is more social."

During scene five, the character of Len brings the baby into a room where Pam, its mother, is in bed. Pam has been neglecting the baby, Len sets it on the edge of the bed with her in order for her to pick it up. She recoils from it, shouting, "Yer goin' mad! It's fallin'! Catch it!" Len then moves the baby so that it is safe. Woodruff remembered how Bond cracked this moment for him: "I was thinking it was about Len's instinct. As soon as she screams, he moves the baby. But Bond said the idea of the moment is like a mini standoff. Like in Brecht's *Caucasian Chalk Circle*, Len can choose at that moment whether he's going to give Pam the opportunity to realize she has an obligation to this child. It might be necessary to hurt the child in that moment and let it fall because then she would have to accept the responsibility."

During scene six, before the baby is killed, members of the gang start to play with the baby and the carriage. The characters of Fred and Pete, however, initially do not take part. Woodruff had staged them to be sitting up against the back wall as the gang shoves the carriage back and forth in front of them. The idea was to point out how Fred and Pete are both watching a horrid event yet taking no action to stop it.

Bond, however, felt strongly that Fred and Pete needed to be on the edge of the stage, facing out into the audience, with the violence happening behind them. Later, Woodruff said, "And he really insisted on it. That opened up something for me. I got out of my own way, my own impositions, my own ideas, and I could see what was really there. It was the idea of seeing Fred and Pete as bystanders looking at the bystandingness of the audience. It was powerful in the room."

He continued, "At some point, you just start trusting him in rehearsal because it's easier to trust genius on some level. You realize he wasn't stuck in time, he just knew. You always give a writer credit for his writing when it's really deserved, when you realize it's not just ramble. Edward's writing is very honed, and the thinking behind each moment is there, and then you, the actors and director, have to find it. It's very exciting to see it."

14.

Wendy Allegaert, who played Liz, a character who appears only in scene ten, struggled with why Liz is even in the play. The role is enigmatic. She comes into a café with the gang of young men, she sits, she smokes, she gives someone change for the jukebox, she gets a cup of coffee, and she is dragged offstage before she can drink more than a few sips. All in all, she speaks only a handful of times, and the lines are short and choppy.

Upon asking Bond if he could give her any clues, he was able to provide her a frame through which to enter Liz. He said, "Liz is, in fact, a metaphor for the whole play. She gives something, she gets something, and in the end, she's deprived."

15.

Leah Gelpe commented, "I discovered that the stark content of the play would tolerate no excess sound information. Bond had written his sound cues with precision and detail. What I had to do was execute the dynamics he laid out as forcefully as possible.

Sometimes the precision of Bond's writing lies in the lack of detail. In scene eleven, the characters Len and Harry fight with a knife over a complete misunderstanding between them. The stage directions are quite ambiguous. It is written that Harry is holding the knife and that Len pulls at and shakes Harry, but then "the knife waves through the air." It is unclear as to what each character's intent is and to what the waving motion should indicate.

In staging the moment, fight choreographer B. H. Barry was asked to help. A heated debate ensued. Barry kept insisting that the actors tell him what their characters' intentions were before giving them movements to try. But the counter possibility was suggested that he give them movements to help the actors discover what their characters' intentions might be.

Labeling the reason for the fight too quickly would mean reducing the scene to merely good versus bad, a clear-cut situation. By structuring the physical score based on Bond's words, a physical exploration could happen into the reason for why the fight occurs. This allows Bond's intentionally ambiguous stage direction to remain so as the actors work toward clarity of their own inner motivations.

16.

The thirteenth and final scene of Saved is silent except for one unimportant line. Four characters execute mundane actions in the same room—fix a chair, read a magazine, clear the table, fill out gambling coupons. After the audience has witnessed the agonizingly violent and frustrating events of the play, they are presented with a scene in which nothing happens. The audience is forced to keep watching.

Edward Bond told us the scene is rhetorical. He said that when we "stand before the paintings of Goya and witness the atrocities recorded there, it is an act of human honor." During scene thirteen, so, too, must the audience honor the events they have just witnessed because "to speak about one's pain is an act of beauty."

Randy Danson recalled a moment in rehearsal when Robert Woodruff and Edward Bond were discussing this notion of forcing an audience to watch these people suffering. Someone in the room made the off-handed remark, "Everybody suffers." Bond then said, "It's true. But in a hundred years, when I'm dead and gone, something bad is going to happen to someone, some pain is going to befall someone, and I want to be able to do something about it."

17.

In a letter to Hanny van der Harst, Bond wrote, "As our societies have deteriorated since [Saved] was written—under the influence of Thatcher and Reagan—I find the play even more relevant than when it was written." Robert Woodruff said, "Globalization has made the play more profound, and less peculiar to London and the British Empire."

As the working classes of the Western world remain voiceless, as the divide between rich and poor continues to grow, as incidents of violence become more prevalent, *Saved* will continue to resonate through the years. On his last day with the company Bond said, "Frankly, I wish I could gather together all the copies of *Saved*, all of the translations in all the different languages, and burn them. Unfortunately, that time has not yet come." ✧

RECOMMENDATIONS

POST ROAD

RECOMMENDATION
KAROO by Steve Tesich

Thomas Beller

A few things about *Karoo*.

It is written in the first person present.

It's author, Steve Tesich, wrote the screenplay for *Breaking Away* which, for some reason, I love.

Karoo is about the consciousness of a bastard, a drinker, a bad father, a stumbler through New Years Day parties in The Dakota, but a benign and in a way a rather lovable bastard who has become afflicted with a disease: he no longer is able to get drunk, even though he drinks a lot.

There is a plot. It is about running into an old flame, about an actress, about a movie but it is entirely beside the point. The point is that the writing is exciting.

Here is a random sample:

> This is a new disease I have picked up. I don't know what to call it. It could either be called a subjectivity disease or an objectivity disease, depending on how you look at it.
>
> The symptoms are always the same.
>
> Despite my nauseating preoccupation with myself, that self seems to slip away rather easily. Try as I might, I am unable to remain subjective about anything for very long. An hour or so, a day or so, a couple of days at best, and my subjectivity leaves me and I move on to begin observing the event in question from some other point of view.
>
> I don't do it on purpose. My mind simply moves on and starts to orbit the event. The event can be a person, an idea, an issue, a heartbreaking letter from my son.

This book is full of short abrupt sentences, and terse little paragraphs of a length one might find in a tabloid, and yet it is somehow a magically linguistic book, its syntax has music, it hops and pops.

I go and pull it off the bookshelf sometimes, just to peruse it and to get jazzed by the language. I go and look at it just for these little language vitamin moments, and then just today I went and looked at it on Amazon. It had been a very ignored book on account of the author dying before it was published. But there on Amazon was a steady stream of excited praise for this book. *Karoo*. I recommend it highly. ✧

Bruno Schultz and Bohumil Hrabal

Myla Goldberg

Talking about just one writer is no fun, so instead I'll babble a bit about two of my favorite dead Eastern Europeans: Bruno Schulz and Bohumil Hrabal. First, Bruno Schulz. There are only two slim collections of short stories— *Street of Crocodiles* and *Sanatorium Under the Sign of the Hourglass*—but boy are they gorgeous. The man spent practically his entire life in the small town of Drohobycz, Poland, a place that, like him, no longer exists. He makes the banal mythic, turning his tailor-father and his shop into a magical, beautiful, and often fearful place with a life of its own. Imaginative, evocative, imagistic, and sensual prose. Though Bohumil Hrabal is probably best known for *Closely Watched Trains,* my two favorites are *Too Loud a Solitude* and *I Served the King of England,* the former about a paper compactor, the latter about a midget who, among other things, works as a waiter during the German occupation of WWII. Both are humorous, dark, human novels which take place in unusual and unexpected corners of existence. Hrabal stays unpredictable, unpretentious, and bitingly smart. Both of these guys have feet firmly in the Kafka camp, another reason I probably like them so much. ✧

RECOMMENDATION

THE ALPHABET IN THE PARK: SELECTED POEMS OF ADELIA PRADO; Translated from the Portuguese by Ellen Watson.

Steve Orlen

Let me drift back to the summer of 1995 and The Grolier Bookstore in Harvard Square where I first encountered the large photograph filling the cover of Ellen Watson's translation of Adelia Prado's *The Alphabet in the Park* (Wesleyan University Press, 1990) . The black and white close-up is of a striking mestizo woman, who seems to grow older and younger as you stare: wide, hooded eyes enlivened by smile lines, and a full, wise and sensual mouth, resonating dimples, and one hand raised to her cheek in what looked like a simultaneous merging of surprise, delight, and immediate understanding of whatever she was beholding at the time. One can fall in love with photographs as well as with poems. I had never heard of Adelia Prado, a middle-aged schoolteacher from the Brazilian mountain town of Minas Gerais. "I am a simple person, a common housewife, a practicing Catholic," she avers in the author's note. Accurate, but as a poet she is now artless, now cunning, pure as a child talking, knowing as a grandmother who used to get in trouble. The poems move as quickly as the jumpy mind of a goofy teenager caught in flagrante delicto. Like the Spanish Surrealists, they develop intuitively and rapidly, and progress, without segue or apparent logic, forward, backward, and laterally. It is the side-step dance that first decorticates then rearranges my mind. "Pieces from a Stained Glass Window" begins:

> Does Japan really exist?
> Or any country I don't know, with its parched coastline?
> What's between the thighs is public. Public and obvious.
> What I want is your heart, the depths of your eyes
> which do everything but speak.
> If you look at me in Spanish, I'll snap my fingers
> and start dancing, dressed in red....

She ends with:

> Just as the saints existed, so does God
> with His unspeakable seductive power.

He's the one who made gold, and gave us the discretion
to invent necklaces to wear around our necks.
Said like that it's so pure I hardly see the sin
in buying one myself.
I've got the same desires as thirty years ago,
immutable as mosquitoes in the sun-drenched kitchen,
my mother making coffee
and my father seated, waiting.

Standing there slowly flipping through the slim volume, I found her opening lines incredibly startling, inviting: "I'm looking for the saddest thing," "Old people spit with absolutely no finesse," "What a fate – that of the flowers/covering the woman in her coffin." The poems are on the one hand down to earth – sensual, sexual, profane, naïve, sophisticated, almost embarrassingly open:

And I am in heat, unceasingly,
I persist in going to the garden to attract butterflies.
   *

I thought sex lasted the whole night
and only at dawn did the bodies part.
The revelation that we are not angels
came to me rather late.

and on the other hand, spiritual. Her Roman Catholicism is only a step away from a paganism which borders on the personal heresy:

Before He knows it, there I am in His lap.
I pull on His white beard.
He throws me the ball of the world,
I throw it back.

Her eye is on love & lust, aging and death, small and large sadnesses, joys, and fears. For immediacy, the poems are always located in a sketch of the actual, "as I roam the neighborhood," and in an abstracting, mosaic imagination, "My soul longs to copulate!" They are essentially enacting and *expressive*: ecstatic, exclamatory, synaesthetic ("A pain this purple induces fainting"), generous ("Poetry will save me, as the purple of flowers/spilling over the fence/absolves the girl her ugly body"). They catalogue by similarity and abrupt shift:

Which is also why

metaphysicians hatch soliloquies,
good governments govern with justice,
and I'm wearing a low-cut dress.

Knowing the poems, sometimes we want to have coffee with the person in whose imagination they were conceived. Lacking the opportunity, we tend to romanticize the lives and careers of The Great Dead poets and the exotic contemporaries. We do it by reduction and surmise. Ellen Watson does so marvelously and succinctly in her introduction:

> Prado's literary career began relatively late—and with a bang—when elder statesman of Brazilian poetry Carlos Drummond de Andrade announced in his Rio de Janeiro newspaper column that Saint Francis was dictating verses to a woman in Minas Gerais. ✧

O.Henry

Michael Snediker

Even before the threat of seeing Uma Thurman and Nick Nolte on its cover, I considered *The Golden Bowl* a pretty fancy accessory. Certainly fancier than the collected short stories of O.Henry, which might still accrue to itself some of the pulp interest of *The Hardy Boys* but is hardly a candidate for nonironic investment. I have, however, as of late (sheepishly, since actually READING O.Henry) changed my mind and decided that loving James wouldn't at all preclude my loving O.Henry, or vice versa. Coming out as an O.Henry lover, I'd like to venture that O.Henry's stories are nonironically moving, not in spite of what are usually impugned as their flaws, but because of them. Yes, these stories were mass-produced (at one point, he was getting paid ten cents a word!), are often one-trick ponies, and are by most standards a feat of self-commodification. Yes, these stories are formulaic. Figure out what sells, find some calculus that articulates this appeal, and you've got one winner after another: this is Danielle Steele, this is John Grisham. In O.Henry, however, this reproducible narrative architecture does something different. There's a gorgeous pathos in reading so many versions of the same story, an abashing wonder at the deadening predictability of his surprise endings. This is a different affective vocabulary than that incited by James, but it is a powerful one nonetheless. Nobody ever wants Isabel Archer to go back to Osmond, but she does, and you can't stop her (though aggravatingly, Jane Campion and Nicole Kidman come close). Isabel's return to Rome is inevitable the way everything in O.Henry is inevitable. O.Henry's characters not only brush up against formal inevitability, they are constituted by it, and one doesn't need to read Foucault to know how *this* feels. The machine-like aspect of O.Henry's writing is in part its most canny virtue. Sixty years before Warhol was producing his Monroe silk screens, O.Henry, whether he knew it or not, was up to a similar game. Reproducibility can be as campy as you like, and as grimly satisfying as a bowl of Cheetos. This pleasure is often lined in O.Henry with a sadness—and even if the candy bar wasn't named after him, who doesn't like a little pleasure lined with sadness? ✧

RECOMMENDATION
James McMichael

Robert Pinsky

James McMichaels's *The World at Large: New and Collected Poems* is published by the University of Chicago Press. It is a great book. In a period when many poets are all trying to be original in the one same way, McMichael is truly and absolutely original, without seeming to fuss or strain at it at all.

His long poem, "Four Good Things" is one of the profound works of our time in any genre.

This writing is not easy, though it is always attractive, and the reward for the reader is the reward of true art. ✧

Five Essential Modern Short Stories
Jaime Clarke

(in no particular order)

1. "Planetarium" by Walter Kirn (*My Hard Bargain.* Knopf, 1990)

The thirteen stories in *My Hard Bargain* are all shot through with Kirn's wonderfully deadpan sense of humor, but "Planetarium" stands out for its compassion toward Karl, the narrator, who admits to the Elder of his church that he is a compulsive masturbator. Elder Johannsen, who is also the coach of the church basketball team (of which Karl is a member), senses that Karl's problem is a team-wide one and puts the team on a "special program" so that the boys can see themselves "the same way God sees you. With clear vision." At the end of this story, in a scene of breathtaking beauty, Karl sees himself, and the others on the team, and stares with wonder at his discovery.

It is a testament to Kirn's abilities as a writer that you forget you're reading a story on a printed page and simply imagine yourself there, sitting on the bench in the locker room, waiting with anticipation for the results of the special program. It is a further testament that the stories in this collection are the rarest tales told: moral stories minus the cloying morality lessons.

2. "Girl With Curious Hair" by David Foster Wallace (*Girl With Curious Hair.* Norton, 1989)

The astute reader will see past the cult of personality that storms around David Foster Wallace and come to discover that he is one of our most inventive—and funniest—storytellers. "Girl With Curious Hair" involves a band of L.A. punkrockers with the unlikely names of Cheese, Tit, Big, Gimlet, Mr. Wonderful, Grope, and Sick Puppy (our faithful narrator), all of whom enjoy a night out at a Keith Jarrett concert. (This story wins hands-down any best first line contest: "Gimlet dreamed that if she did not see a concert last night she would become a type of liquid, therefore my friends Mr. Wonderful, Big, Gimlet and I went to see Keith Jarrett play a piano concert at the Irvine Concert Hall in Irvine last night." The story also wins—again hands-down--any best last line contest, too.) The narrator recounts with hilarious affectlessness his standing as a Young Republican, his family background, and how he came to be associated with his current roster of friends. (Oh, and there's his affinity for his gold lighter.) And when Gimlet spots a girl with curious hair a few rows ahead of them in the Irvine Concert Hall, the story really takes off.

These characters could have been sired by Anthony Burgess, but the way David Foster Wallace turns a phrase inside out, "Girl With Curious Hair" stands alone, without predecessor or progeny.

3. "Lawns" by Mona Simpson. (*The Iowa Review,* 1985. Reprinted in *The Best American Short Stories 1986,* edited by Raymond Carver. Houghton Mifflin Company, 1986)

A writing instructor in college assigned this story for, among other things, its wonderful first line: "I steal." (When you're learning how to write fiction, you learn that first lines and last lines are awfully important-- and you're baffled at how to write good ones, but running up and down this list I see that all these stories are great examples of how it's done.) Once past the first line, though, the reader quickly gathers that this story is remarkable for its ability to humanize a character with a terrible secret, to portray a victim without relying on the conventional trappings of victimization. Jenny is a freshman pre-med major at Berkeley who has a roommate (Lauren), a job working Saturdays in the campus mailroom (which is the scene of her thefts), and a great new boyfriend (Glenn) whose job it is to mow the lawns on campus. Jenny has also been molested by her father since she was eight. Sound like an afterschool special? In the hands of a less-skilled writer it easily could be, but Simpson effectively portrays the unspeakable emotions victims of molestation must feel. And if that weren't remarkable enough, Simpson goes one step further and creates a sympathetic molester in Jenny's father, who shows up in Jenny's dorm room unannounced, reservations made at a nearby hotel, ready for a weekend with his lover. Jenny's father is actually in love with her, complicating matters for Jenny, and complicating the narrative with complex emotions. For obvious reasons, readers (and people in general) yearn for the molester to wear the black hat. Our need to hate an unlikable character, or a likable character that behaves in an unlikable manner, comforts us, and we're grateful when the author provides us with this cover. Which is what makes "Lawns" so much more unsettling.

4. "This Is Us, Excellent" by Mark Richard (*The Ice at the Bottom of the World.* Knopf, 1989)

It probably isn't fair—or prudent—to try to choose a single story of the ten collected in this remarkable book (which won the 1990 PEN/Hemingway Foundation Award and features The Best American selection "Strays"), but for the reader who has a predilection for voice fiction, "This Is Us, Excellent" scratches that itch. Richard's powers are such that he manages to both horrify and entertain the reader with what is ostensibly a tale of domestic violence. Told through the voice of the nameless older brother, the story recounts the exploits of two brothers whose father beats their mother and exiles the family to Psycho Za, a local pizza parlor, for a Manic Size Train Wreck 'za—extra everything—and a side of Logjam Fries while he watches sports at home in peace. The poetics of the story are such as to render the brothers as knowing and naïve at the same time (The older brother defends his old man to an inquisitive school nurse: "I told them our dad can beat up whoever he wants to."), and the reader has the feeling that once the boys see their life as more than an episode of "Danger: Duke McQuaid"—their favorite TV show—they will simply become another staggering statistic, broken like the arm of the man who runs the Rocket Sling, a favorite ride at the local amusement park, who is forever resting his arm under the errant clutch handle that always slips.

5. "Pretty Judy" by Kevin Canty. (A Stranger in this World. Doubleday, 1994)

The centerpiece of this collection is "The Victim," an ultra-grim story about a boyfriend and girlfriend who are involved in an auto accident with a stranger leaving a bar and who are, in turn, lured back to the stranger's mobile home, blown on its side from a storm, ostensibly to get paid. Needless to say, the couples' lives are changed irreparably. "The Victim" showcases Canty's talents well--and the ten stories in the collection are all gems--but "Pretty Judy" is a story remarkable not just for its portrayal of the accidental perversion of innocence, but also for Canty's gift at rendering a moment--and characters--with fresh, realistic detail. Judy MacGregor lives in "a white house with green shutters in a lake of brilliant lawn" on Paul's street and calls down from her perch high above to anyone who walks by. The neighborhood kids know very little about Judy, other than she's big and older than her age. Maybe nineteen, maybe twenty-one. And that she's retarded. One afternoon, Judy calls Paul up to her room. As Paul tiptoes through the empty house, empty except for what waits for him on the second floor, he has no idea what he's going to discover about himself in the colorful confines of Judy's room. Judy is surprisingly compliant and pulls Paul to the floor, her pink jumpsuit with the giant sun on the front quickly balled up next to them. Paul dashes out of the house, fearing discovery, and it isn't until he realizes he's left his tennis racquet in Judy's room that he knows he'll be back.

And then he can't stop thinking of Judy.

And then he can't stop thinking he should do the right thing.
So he plans a date, an afternoon at the zoo.

One of the beautiful aspects of this story is Canty's pairing a narrator trying to puzzle his way through adolescence with a character who has no perception, either of the world within or the world without. Paul quickly realizes the visit to the zoo was a mistake since Judy has no discernible appreciation for the trip; and he starts to realize how big of a mistake it really is when Judy spots a group of retarded children and panics, thinking she'll be made to go with them. But ever the burgeoning romantic, Paul makes one last go of it, assenting to Judy's wish to go on a boat ride in a small lake at the zoo. You'll have to read the last line to find out what happens. ✧

DANGEROUS MUSE: THE LIFE OF LADY CAROLINE BLACKWOOD, by Nancy Schoenberger

Liam Rector

Nancy Schoenberger's biography, *Dangerous Muse: The Life of Lady Caroline Blackwood* (Nan A. Talese/Doubleday, $27.50 cloth), is a splendid book for anyone interested in literature, painting, class, Anglo-Irish life, American-British life, beauty, booze, history, aging, poetry, and any number of other things.

Dangerous Muse is essentially the story of writer and Guinness heir Caroline Blackwood, wife of painter Lucien Freud (Freud's grandson), friend to painter Francis Bacon, and the final wife of poet Robert Lowell. Blackwood's novels and nonfiction books are renowned for their satire suffused with a nihilism that is unflinching, specializing in unsympathetic character and characters.

For anyone interested in the Lowell lineage in American poetry this book is an absolute field day, comparable in many ways to David Larkin's recent *Partisans*. Both books are Gossip of a Very High Order, intravenously shot through with a matter-of-fact hipness, spareness, speed, and razzle-dazzle, operating at great depths and picking up what's important along the way. (History itself is gossip of a High, Middle, and Low order.) Both books have an excellent feel for both the life and times, and Schoenberger's book has an especial grasp of the role of sheer money. No aristocratic variation on the boho from Soho character has been so well sketched since Tom Wolfe.

The photographs of Caroline Blackwood in *Dangerous Muse* are one of the more eerie aspects of the book. I found myself, as I read, returning to these photographs over and over. Blackwood goes from an early ravenous beauty, captured in photographs by Walker Evans, to a kind of Audenesque face on which time and hard living have had full play. This narrative of beauty is deeply ingrained not only in Blackwood's face but in Schoenberger's story of Blackwood's life. Beauty not only fades; in the mind, spirit, and body of Caroline Blackwood it slashes and tears, though it finally stands up with a kind of stoical, macabre dignity of character.

Poet Frank Bidart is quite interestingly one of Schoenberger's main sources on Lowell, and Schoenberger has conducted quite her own study of unsympathetic character in *Dangerous Muse*. ✦

RECOMMENDATION
Winton, Munro, Berger

Frederick Reiken

Why is that no one has ever heard of the 1992 novel *Cloudstreet* by
Australian writer Tim Winton? Lyrical and compassionate, with moments
of subtle, radiant magic, this big, rollicking, deeply felt book tells the story
of two families who co inhabit a large house in the coastal town of Perth,
Western Australia. The sense of place is exquisite, with a landscape that
comes to seem as palpable as the characters. It is one of my favorite novels
of all time.

Winton has won every Australian award there is, and his follow-up to
Cloudstreet, a solid but far less ambitious book entitled *The Riders*, was a
finalist for the Booker Prize in 1995. His novels sell like crazy in other coun-
tries, but here they barely stay in print. George Stade, reviewing *The Riders*
for the *New York Times Book Review* in 1995, stated that he did not believe
that we are "ready" for Tim Winton in this country, though he didn't really
manage to explain why.

Winton followed *The Riders* with a children's book called *Blueback*, a
fablistic tale about a boy's friendship with a giant grouper, which, charming
as it was, was not exactly a career move. But I offer this as an even greater
incentive to explore his work – the fact that Winton seems a writer of rare
authenticity, lacking pretense or preoccupation with self-promotion. I first
heard of him because I attended a reading at UC Irvine while I was in graduate school. It was one of those readings that no one bothered to publicize,
so at the last minute the reading series organizer raced around the English
and Comp. Lit. building begging everyone she encountered in the hallways
to fill the twenty empty chairs. Winton didn't seem fazed, though he did
give one of the most uninspired readings I've ever heard. Admittedly, I
didn't buy the book until two years later, when I found it remaindered,
though I subsequently returned to the store and bought ten more remaindered copies, which I distributed among relatives and friends. Since then I
have been buying up used copies, as publisher Graywolf managed to let the
book go out of print in record time.

Two years ago I learned that fellow Australian Jane Campion optioned
the *Cloudstreet* film rights and that around the same time Geoffrey Rush
optioned *The Riders*, so perhaps Hollywood will resurrect Tim Winton,
though I doubt it. In the meantime, pick up *Cloudstreet*, no matter how
hard you have to search (or write me and I'll send you one of my copies).

A second book on my list of lesser-known literary marvels is by Alice Munro, who certainly is not a writer who has been quietly overlooked. Yet while everyone and their cousin is busy selecting "Meneseteung" or "Friend of My Youth" for their latest *Best Since the Big Bang* anthology, it seems that these days no ever mentions *The Beggar Maid* (1977), a book of interconnected stories that is also one of my all-time favorites.

The ten stories span the life of protagonist Rose, who starts out as a young girl in a poor small town in rural Ontario and, following a failed marriage and the loss of custody of her daughter, goes on to achieve her own equivocal success, first as a television talk show host and then as an actress, despite never coming to terms with—or else precisely because she has never come to terms with—any sense of her own identity (the book was originally published under the title *Who Do You Think You Are?*) The psychological precision is unnerving and the arc of Rose's transformations no less than masterful, but what is most unsettling about this book is the manner in which Munro, within and between stories, has crafted an entirely nonlinear tapestry of a narrative that, by using the interconnected story technique, sustains a laser-like focus even as she jumps at will between the different contexts and time frames of Rose's life. Munro has practically invented her own novelistic form in *The Beggar Maid*, and overall the book is simply a wonder.

Finally, I mention the British author and art critic John Berger and will boldly recommend exploring his entire body of work. You can usually find at least a dozen books by Berger in any bookstore. They range from his 1972 Booker Prize-winning novel, *G.*, to his most recent novel, *King*, neither of which I loved. What I have loved are the following: the story cycle "The Three Lives of Lucie Cabrol" in the collection *Pig Earth;* the long title story of the collection Once in Europa; the novel *To the Wedding*; the essays "That Which is Held," "Ape Theatre," and "Lost Off Cape Wrath" in Keeping a Rendezvous; the essay "Appearances" in *Another Way of Telling*; and the essay "The White Bird" in The Sense of Sight. I'd recommend starting out with the book *Ways of Seeing*, a series of essays that grew out of a BBC series and has become a staple in many art history 101 classes. It introduces some of Berger's major themes and concerns, and if you like it you can go on to another book. Perhaps my favorite of his works is his meditation on time and space and art and love and death and absence, entitled *And Our Faces, My Heart, Brief as Photos*. While the poems interspersed within this 100-page volume are a bit didactic, his analytical musings on the "work" of van Gogh's art, the "labor" of poetry, and the non-Euclidean time dimensions we inhabit daily are sublime. Here is one of my favorite passages, about the fundamentally human problem of absence:

> The visible implies an eye. It is the stuff of the relation between seen and seer. Yet the seer, when human, is conscious of what his eye cannot and will never see because of time and distance. The visible both includes him (because he sees) and excludes him (because he is not omnipresent). The visible consists for him of the seen which, even when it is threatening, confirm his existence. To this human ambiguity of the visible one then has to add the visual experience of absence, whereby we no longer see what we saw. We face a disappearance. And a struggle ensues to prevent what has disappeared, what has become invisible, falling into the negation of the unseen, defying our existence. Thus, the visible produces faith in the reality of the invisible and provokes the development of an inner eye which retains and assembles and arranges, as if in an interior, as if what has been seen may be forever partly protected against the ambush of space, which is absence.

Thirty years ago or so, Berger was perhaps the most important art critic in Europe. He now resides and works in a small peasant village in the French Alps, living among the people he has championed in many of his books. As for why he hasn't won a Nobel Prize, your guess is as good as mine. I suspect it has something to do with his Marxist political leanings, which show up regularly in his work, often quietly, as he's analyzing, say, the manner in which authenticity depends on remaining faithful to the fundamental ambiguity of experience. But whether your politics match or not, Berger's concerns are so multidimensional that there's no way to pigeonhole his arguments. He is a writer of unclassifiable innovation. ❖

RECOMMENDATION
THE BOOK OF DISQUIET by Fernando Pessoa

Anne McCarty

Fernando Pessoa, a Portuguese poet born in the late-nineteenth century who wrote in a schizophrenic style by creating a variety of pseudonyms he called "heteronyms," also wrote prose in a book titled *The Book of Disquiet*. Pessoa chose to write this text solely in the guise of Bernard Soares, the heteronym with a fictive biography closest to Pessoa's life. He commented that Soares "appears whenever I'm tired or sleepy, when my powers of ratiocination and my inhibitions are slightly suspended; that prose is a constant daydreaming."

The book is a diary of his daydreams—he may offer the occasion that triggered his thoughts, but these moments never combine into a narrative, instead leading him into musing and venting his abundant anxiety that is tempered only by love for Lisbon, writing, and certain moments, what he calls "my history without life." In the short, dated entries, he details his love for the city, the puddles and peddlers in the street, the river Tagus, feelings that bring him to conclude "[t]he artificial is the path that brings us closer to the natural," one of his many near proverbs. They're the best parts of the book. Another one: "He who makes his existence monotonous is wise because then every small incident has the privilege of being a marvel." Yes, he tells himself, my boring life has allowed for a rich interior life. Who hasn't needed this logic at some time?

Though his tone can become whiny, Pessoa writes frequently with a humor that shines through the haze of time and translation (be sure to read the Alfred Mac Adam translation), making his anxiety almost charming. He's the poster boy for what was emerging as the modern personality, the underground man. Writing with a self-deprecation that's hard to beat, his pose as eiron eventually balloons into an alazon until it bursts back into the deflated man. According to Pessoa's logic, only by working in his small office at a mindless job of bookkeeping can he be the great poet, but then he admits that the poet is no better than the baker. And his variations of self-deflation, followed by inflation, affects how he sees the world: from both below and above. His boss, Vasques, figures heavily in the book, and he, like most of the people who appear in these pages, is alternately adored and scorned by Pessoa. As a man tortured by his own thoughts and sensitivity "I always think about and pay attention to two things at once" he envies what he views as the simplicity of others, then chastises himself for thinking he is above anyone. He is self-aware enough to know what self-awareness leads to.

The book is a catalogue of the inconsistencies possible in one man.

After reading something he had written in French long ago, Pessoa hardly recognized himself: "I continuously feel that I was someone else... What is this space between myself and myself? [...] here is something beyond the other than the mere flow of personality between its own banks: there is the other absolute, another being that was mine. A being who, as I grew older, lost imagination, emotion, a type of intelligence, a way of feeling things [...] On which bank am I standing if I see myself in the depths?" He never felt remotely like a consistent or identifiable figure. Still, he attempted to get outside himself, to get a break from himself, only to be lead further into introspection. And if he has no self, how can he escape? (Critics love to point out that the word Pessoa means "person.") All this is fascinating to watch and points to how bizarre identity issues can be, especially for writers.

At one point he asserts that writing is better than living, at other moments, that writing is living. Though little may be known about the more personal aspects of Pessoa's life, and little revealed here, what he thought reveals more than what he did. ✧

CRITICISM

POST ROAD

Why Baltimore House Music Is The New Dylan

Scott Seward

I.

There are superstar pop-cult icons beloved by millions who were or are meaner, nastier, and more spiteful than Bob Dylan (your mom for instance—followed closely by the likes of Lucille Ball, Billy Joel, Paul Simon, and Bill Cosby), but he's within spitting distance of the head of the pack. An idiot windbag and bully from the git-go, his tooth & nail-filled words (his tongue on fire like liar's pants) simultaneously function as self-righteous harangues aimed at everyone who doesn't get it/ain't us/isn't in the know—wake up calls for any Mr. or Mrs. Jones-to-be who feels that their freedom is impinged upon by the responsibilities and duties thrown at them by, you know, church/state/manifest destiny/gym teachers/etc.— and as hyper-literate (though often clouded with beatnik bombast and trickster whatzits) revenge fantasies designed not only to comfort bespectacled boys wronged by girls from the right counties but to also assuage the fears of those people who worry that the right fingers will not be pointed at people on the wrong side.

Early Dylan fans, not content with the murder balladeers and chain gang troubadours of previous generations, understandably wanted a blowhard to call their own. And as the thinking person's Elvis, Dylan single-handedly trumped the Depression-era love of hard work, war wounds, craftsmanship and dirt with youth, wit, and a cool-ass hair-do (his kinky rooster-cut, for example, working as many angles and directions as his creativity at that time). Dylan's early appropriation of a dustbowl vocalese and aesthetic (what could be more natural for a 20-year-old kid from the sticks then to sound like a black-lunged miner with miles of bad road behind him) may have been borne out of a deep and abiding love for dead and dying rail-riding pinkos, but more realistically it was his ticket into a burgeoning folk scene always on the lookout for sympathetic fellow travelers who would show the proper respect for the decrepit elders and originators of La Vie de Hootenanny.

Once he was through genuflecting at Woodie Guthrie's bedside (and getting patted on the head by the story-song master) and using his Midwestern wiles to get into Joan Baez's back pages (she the shining young star pre-Bob), he had made his mark and could proceed to do what he did. Which was: ruin everything! He was too cool! He was punk as fuck! His sneer was a mile wide! He raised the bar too high! His songs were too good! He looked really cute in pointy boots! He corrupted The Beatles! He made rock "important"! And "serious"! He subjected the world to thousands of horrible singersongwritercountryrockstreamofconsciousnessbrooding-badpoetry bands! He made people who had no business playing the blues play the blues! He was too big for rock, and ever after people wanted to be bigger than rock without ever realizing that rock is plenty big enough already for whatever they could add to it. (In honoring his 60th year to walk among mortals, His Royal Sleepy Bobness has been the indifferent recipient of a cavalcade of articles, books, monographs, and commemorative trading cards designed with an eye toward superlative-whiplash and reaffirmation of the myths that followed him on the road to sainthood.) Rock before Dylan was mostly fun and then it wasn't (because of him), and it mostly isn't now (because of him). And the rock & roll that most people love does not have as much to do with him (it has more to do with Chuck Berry), and thus to listen to this rock & roll is usually a lot more fun. As a rule, people who don't listen to Bob Dylan are usually a lot more fun to hang out with. Having said that, everyone should own at least four Bob Dylan albums (*The Freewheelin' Bob Dylan, Highway 61 Revisited, Blood on the Tracks,* and *Desire* will do).

It is funny that the only people who actually approached the ferocity of early pre-motorbike crash Dylan (1966 being the dividing line between scary can-do-no-wrong Dylan and bloody, beaten, bowed, sometimes scary, and good-when-he-feels-like-it Dylan) were the art brut garage and punk bands of the 60's and 70's. The dandies and aesthetes of those eras mainly pegged the corn pone/po'boy/nasal/fake Carter family/should sound like you're 60 when you're 20/spaghetti western Dylan that he could get away with because he was and is a freak of nature and because he invented the shit in the first place. That ferocity was hunger and could previously be heard on Charles Ives and Eartha Kitt records, making it alien to most pop and pop-folk fans at the time. The juvenile delinquents heard Dean and Brando in his voice, but unfortunately his words were too good and the boring people heard Shakespeare.

2.

You can't blame Louis Armstrong for Kenny G, can you? (Yes, you can.) Sheryl Crow, Thalia Zedek, Lucinda Williams, Iris Dement, and Chan Marshall are all pretty rockin', and they wouldn't sound or be the same without a little Dylan in them. Right? Right, but they would have been fine without him, too. The problem lies with the egghead factor: namely, those folks who demand that rock-based forms must invoke more chin-stroking than hip-shaking (so that anything worthwhile must be accompanied by charts, time-lines, genealogical surveys, A + B = C). And so, so what? The fun stuff sells by the ton. Singer/songwriter, roots-rock, alt-country, and the like have smaller audiences and are often ignored by the public no matter how many rave reviews an Aimee Mann or Steve Earle album gets. So why the hubbub, bub?

Certain people see it as a travesty that cottage industries like Mann and Earle don't get their due and sell like hotcakes (even though they sell fine in comparison to those put-everything-they-own-in-the-back-of-a-station-wagon-for-the-gig-in-Duluth road warrior folkies and hometown blue-grass champs with talent and flair by the bait-bucketful but no business savvy, high cheekbones or colorful stories of their days on junk or in stir). And what these people refuse to grasp is that Dylan-inspired past-glory-obsessed art-song pop forms are too rarefied and in love with their own purity to connect with a world at large that for the most part revels in the here and now of the time in which they live.

In other words, Sleater-Kinney is for connoisseurs and people who take music seriously as hobby and theory and connect-the-dots art/history appreciation (i.e. people with a lot of free time on their hands). Sleater-Kinney fans (or Ani Difranco or Wilco fans) are by and large either smart white kids or smart white adults who care little for the reasons why 95% of the world doesn't give a shit about Sleater-Kinney. And they, for the most part, view what 95% of the world listens to and loves as trash, fad, kitsch, camp, eye-rolling nonsense, an annoyance, an anthropological/sociological abstraction, or a reason to move to the suburbs. They, like early Dylan fans, think that what they like is the best because they are smarter at making nec-essarily false distinctions between what is "real" music and what is "fake" music. This would be fine, and well-educated white kids and adults should be free to live in a world where poetic white guitar-strummers serenade them through the travails of their white existence, but unfortunately this myopia extends to the mainstream media (educated white-folks radio, magazines and newspapers), which is why you still get five articles about Aimee Mann not being able to find an audience/sympathetic record com-pany/shoes that fit instead of five articles about something that might res-onate culturally with a larger group of citizens (something significant to people beyond Aimee's fine fan-base—really, there is nothing wrong with Aimee Mann—I'm sure she's a lovely person). The *New York Times* and oth-ers act as if the world is breathlessly waiting for news about the current state of such innovative and modern art forms as alternative folk/alterna-tive rock/alternative country music. It is not. But these rags know their audience. If another rapper goes on trial maybe they will be able to slip in a paragraph about his/her artistic process somewhere. Think about this: rap has been one of the most explosive, revolutionary, artistic, and culturally significant forms of music to appear in decades. When was the last time you read an article or account in any mainstream forum about how a particular hip-hop artist actually "made" an album or song? It is as if rap music just falls from the trees onto Jay-Z's head already fully formed. And on the other hand, how many full-page reviews are there of a new Eric Clapton album that explain in detail how it sounds exactly like every other Eric Clapton album?

When it comes to music, how do you write about things that are timely and culturally significant? Does it involve asking Joni Mitchell how she feels about Eminem? Probably not. Does it involve asking people in Indonesia how they feel about Eminem? Maybe. You would probably get some pretty interesting ideas from an Indonesian Eminem fan. You might actually open yourself up to all kinds of questions about cross-pollinization, language, translation, influences, politics - the sky's the limit. Joni would probably shrug and say she hated his small-mindedness or loved his poetic expressions of rage. Same goes for critics. It's mostly either/or, thumbs up/thumbs down, and rarely why, or how.

Petty, parochial, small-minded. Conservative. Ambivalent and dismissive of any genre that falls outside of their comfort zone. Lost in the past. (And hey, the past is great to get lost in. You could listen to ancient jug bands for years without ever leaving your armchair. The past is the healthy recipient of a lot of modern critical energy. If there's a long dead fiddler with one recording to his name he's no doubt getting fully annotated, researched and box-setted for your enjoyment as we speak. Which is fine, because lost banjo gods need their day in the sun and every minute we are reminded of someone else who slipped through the cracks. But, meanwhile, in the real world, thriving amidst a nation of mods are future dead legends of all shapes and sizes. And some of them don't sound like The Wallflowers. Realizing the easy irony, it still never fails to amaze that Bob Dylan's son is in a band that sounds like it was inspired by bands who were inspired by Bob Dylan. It is enough to make your head spin.)

These are common traits of a lot of the people writing the history books (so to speak) on modern music. Every once in a while, a fad catches their eye. If three French disco albums come out in the same month, then there is talk of a French disco boom. When Paul Simon went to Africa, we were inundated with a lot of bad African music. Hey, thanks! Other than that, it is the same old, same old. Next big things, flavor of the day, new Beatles, new Dylans. What is something new that sounds reassuringly like something old? Let's write about that! Let's dismiss everything that people love as a fad and call it garbage that will go away and be replaced with new garbage without ever wondering why people love it and what it means to them. Let's do this forever. Let's make it really difficult for new things to grow. We just know, even though it's been going strong since 1979, that rap will go away, because we don't like it! (Or don't want to really listen to it. Because listening to new sounds is too much work.)

Things aren't that bad, are they? Maybe not. There are certainly more spots now where people can get the word out and offer good critical writing about things that get glossed over or ignored by traditional outlets. There are plenty of great, thoughtful writers who are omnivorous and democratic if you know where to look for them. Freaks, fans, and scholars abound on-line. Most mainstream mags and papers, however, lean toward the horrible. And those are the sources that people are more apt to actually read. Maybe it all comes down to this: a day when cultural conservatives all step down and everyone else just refuses to write a review for a new Rod Stewart album. (Unless he makes a concept album about his penis or something, is there even any point? "Honey, the paper says the new Rod Stewart is less than stellar." "Hmm.. should we buy it then?" "Gee, I don't know...'Less than Stellar'...that doesn't sound like our Rod!")

3.

Realizing that the search for "the new Dylan" is an old joke does not discount the fact that people look for new heroes who resemble the old ones. And if you had to pick one person to fit that truth, justice, American way/voice of a generation suit that Dylan wore it would probably be Bruce Springsteen, although in some ways you could say he was the anti-Dylan. He is inclusive and warmer. He hasn't screwed with his fans the way Dylan has in too many cringe-worthy ways to mention. For the most part, he gives the people what they want. The height of his treachery to the working-stiff shtick was being married at one time to a supermodel and moving to California. But, all in all, he does not seem much changed over the years. Still plays a godawful club in Jersey every once in a while. Still throws bones to the bar band that he rode in on. Springsteen connects with his audience in the same way that Dylan did (and does). They both strive (Springsteen in conscious imitation) for that epic, dusty, lone gunman appeal, and they are both pretty good at it.

Where things get tricky is with the "spokesman for a generation" thing. Whether they asked for it or not, they both got it. But without bursting anyone's Brotherhood of Man bubble, it has got to be said that not a whole lot of black or Latino (or any other minority in this country) people ever listened to Bruce or Bob that much. You can go to one of their concerts if you don't believe it. And if we are talking musical legacy, there were very few black artists who needed anything from Dylan to get ahead artistically, which is no "big deal," really—but is just another example of "separate but equal." I'm guessing some people would call Roberta Flack, Phoebe Snow, Ritchie Havens, Garland Jeffries, Tracey Chapman and Jeffrey Gaines black Dylans. And Prince, who probably comes closest to "being" Bob Dylan. These people all had their moments, but none of them were ever that revolutionary (not that they were trying to be). Prince certainly had revolution-ary uses for the color purple, but he really did not break existing rules, or create new ones in his image (and, come to think of it, the 1985 soundtrack to the movie "The Color Purple" may have been more radical than anything Prince himself ever came up with). He was and is simply a supremely talented entertainer who made the 80s more bearable. Gil Scott-Heron created new sounds with his sermonizing proto-rap mixed with jazz and funk, but social justice—not great songs—was his first concern.

When you talk about people who carry on someone's legacy of musical exploration and social impact, dividing would-be heirs by race is just silly. Who had the most on their generation: Marvin Gaye or Loudon Wainwright III? There you go. And if you say that a new Dylan *has* to be an adenoidal out-of-tune harmonica-muncher, then there is no room for argument. But if you say that the new Dylan is someone who is not afraid to reflect the world around them with biting vigor (or vigorous biting), to shock with the new and cut right through the bland in the hopes of making a new land for everyone, well then that could be anyone. Parliament/Funkadelic were the new Dylan and no one even cared. N.W.A. were the new Dylan, but they shocked virgin ears and people would not listen. Public Enemy would have been the new Dylan if it weren't for Flava Flav (on second thought, perhaps his malevolent tricksterism added the crucial element that would make them true heirs to the throne). Countless pale male singer/strummers have been foisted on the public since Dylan's arrival, at the expense of really groovy sounds that didn't fit the mold(iness), the close-minded parochialism of classic rock snobs having propped up lesser lights for years on the basis that they have some slight surface resemblance to that special someone of greater talent. Come to think of it, wasn't Bob Marley the new Dylan? Oh no, that's right, Steve Forbert was. Let's just belabor the point into the ground once more with a sledgehammer: if it were up to *Rolling Stone*, we would all be listening to the Long Ryders, Jason & the Scorchers, the Bodeans, the Cruzados, Green on Red, Uncle Tupelo, Wilco, Son Volt and Wallflowers records until the day we die. If you search for pasty-faced folk-rockers you will find a mess of them. If you search for something that bewilders and scares you with its newness, you might just find the next Bob Dylan.

Someday, someone will write the People's History of Music in America, and it won't include the Band or the Byrds. It would include the people that those groups mugged for their overalls and moonshine jugs (as well as the inventors of the Swim, the Hucklebuck and the Electric Slide). Until then, people should not be intimidated by some snooze-rock orthodoxy and bow to that judgment. If you think the Pixies or Modest Mouse or your Aunt Minnie are the greatest rock bands in history, go tell it on the mountain.

Give your version of events. Frederic Jameson says in *The Political Unconscious:* "History can be apprehended only through its effects, and never directly as some reified force. This is indeed the ultimate sense in which History as ground and untranscendable horizon needs no particular theoretical justification: we may be sure that its alienating necessities will not forget us, however much we might prefer to ignore them."[1] In other words, don't be afraid to fuck with history, because history isn't afraid to fuck with you. The new Dylan should be anyone or anything worth a damn. Anything of your time that gives the finger to a metaphorical Pete Seeger (although I'm sure he's a lovely man). The Sex Pistols were the new Dylan (for a day or two). And without a doubt, the Baltimore House music scene is one of the greatest new Dylans to appear in years.

4.

Baltimore House is the sound of war. As music, it is deadly, ferocious, and filled with ten thousand tensions all vying for your uneasiness. Like good folk or blues music, you wonder how something so simple could be so effective. The more you listen, the more you begin to make crazy judgments like this: the best music really is music made for dancing! Alternately called "ghetto trax," "Baltimore trax," "Doo Dew," or "Urban House," depending on who you are talking to, it is dance music for gangstas with A.D.D. Break beats, heavily processed drum tracks, and vocal samples. That's it, really. The odd synth sample pops up, but the simple repetition of kick drums on top of ancient beats on top of yet another layer of bass-heavy drums on top of a single phrase or exhortation repeated vocally *ad nauseum* is all there is to it. Sounds appetizing, no? Its origins can be found in old Miami Bass, D.C. Go-Go and Hip-Hop/House music crossovers of the late 8os/early 90s. But the formula employed by these Baltimore (and odd DC) DJs and producers is wholly their own. It's a micro-genre, barely a blip on the national dance music radar. But in the simple homegrown formula that it has cooked up, there are a multitude of variations on a theme.

Baltimore trax is hypnotic in ways that a lot of music that aims for hypnotic effect rarely is. Maybe it is just the frenetic pace or the energy, but it is *wide-awake* trance music. It is also definitely not for everybody. But then a lot of high-tech modern dance music surely isn't, because it demands attention, which is something casual music listeners can not always muster. Great techno, house music, and disco always reminded me of great Indian music. The more you give in the more you get out of it. That's why a lot of rock listeners have a problem with dance music and see it all as indistinguishable wallpaper: they are used to being fed the experience through a

[1] *The Political Unconscious: Narrative as a Socially Symbolic Act. Ithaca: Cornell University Press, 1981, page 102*

Pavlovian repetition of what they have come to expect from bass, drums, guitar, vocal. Rock fans in general are usually much less discriminating listeners than any other music fan. (Not that mainlining power chords and riffs ain't a hell of a lot of fun—it is!)

Unlike rock music, the identity of the performers is virtually non-existent, taking a complete back seat to the music whose job it is to rock clubs, cars and bodies. Who makes the greatest trax tracks? Drag queens, apparently. Who else? DJ Class, DJ Technics, Dukeyman, Booman, Rod Lee. Collectively, they add up to greatness. If you are curious enough to seek out some prime crabtown tracks, any compilation on the Unruly label will serve that purpose. Anything by the likes of Scottie B., Sixth Sense or Spice is worth your hard-earned dough (so search the web or move to Baltimore for more info.)

Listening to this music at home can sometimes be a claustrophobic experience unless you live in a gymnasium or ballroom. It's so tight and tense with every second of sound seemingly ready to burst at the seams and fry your player. Or not. It all depends on the listener. Like early Detroit techno, it sometimes has the dry air of dead cities breathing down your neck. The humor and calls to arms, the dogs barking, and disco whistles, the ripped-off samples (Spiderman, the Taxi theme, Destiny's Child, sped-up Michael Jackson, Outkast, Fat Albert, electropop classic Din Da Da), the local yokel shout-outs to Baltimore hoods, the fighting and fucking. None of it drowns out some weird sense of loneliness in-between the beats. In-between the energy and invention. Is there such a thing as poignant booty music? Can there be pathos in a song called "Flowers II Hoes," whose vocal consists of the one line "I give flowers to all my hoes"? How about "It's my pussy and I'll do what I want, I'm a big girl now!" repeated until the sassy explicitness of the line turns into a mantra? That heady mix of fear, sweat, exhilaration and maniacal use of percussion (and the thrill of hearing somebody make something out of nothing and making nothing swing so damn hard) creates an urban aural nightmare that many hardcore hipster headz and knob-twiddling doofuses could only dream of making.

Some would call Baltimore house music mindless, but that is just another word for transcendent. It is high on its own invention. It juggles the desire for self-expression inherent in going public with the just-as-strong desire to spit in your face. That the personal as political is wound tightly around a sound that, though having obvious roots in the past, remains a monster wholly unto itself. Within that sound resides the unspoken but palpable belief that there is redemption only through more music and more nights (this is what Baltimore house music *and* Bob Dylan mean to me.) It exists right now with an aesthetic, language, and set of rules that work as long as everyone agrees that it works, and when it does not work anymore, it will become something else. Making history does not seem to be the point. Making people move seemed to be the only point, but on the way to that something weird and wild happened. The scene became a universe unto itself. To paraphrase "the bard": They've got everything they need, they're artists, and they don't look back. Some would call it noise and they would have a point because it is noisy as hell. But sometimes the sound of people throwing a party to impress their neighbors and wake the dead is one of the only ways that we are reminded that we have neighbors and that we are not, in fact, dead.

People who believe that any music aimed at the groin or the dance floor is somehow inferior to the artier or more self-consciously (or more seriously yearning or yawningly serious) poetic forms have poetic sticks up their self-conscious asses. Of course, only eggheads believe this, and they are pretty easy to avoid. But, thanks to all their talk of dumbing down and lo-com-denoms (as if radio and television obviously skewed toward kiddie dollars is evidence of the decline of western civ), they have managed to be pretty persuasive in their arguments that a culture is doomed if it lauds disposable pop music (which is often more enlightening than stuff that aims for enlightenment by shining light on the dark corners of our inner lives through impressionistic snapshots of daily life in spare, minimal language fraught with the unspoken workings of the heart), at the expense of the often dead-end sludge they posit as so stately, literate and valuable.

Dylan's great achievement was making a new sound that had not existed before him which effortlessly blended levels of the confessional personal (a style that did not exist in song before him other than in a more prosaic form, by the originators and authors of folk and blues standards) with the chronic malcontent's belief that along with the rest of the world he was being played for a sucker. (For the first time in Technicolor, a whole nation's unease and malaise was writ large with a honk heard round the globe.) Bob Dylan might have a lot to answer for (he must have known what he was unleashing on an innocent white bread world!), but not nearly as much as those bloated, hysterical guardians of a sickly, second-hand, and stolen mythology based on bastardized rock & roll idioms, which exist solely for the benefit of the complacent and nostalgic consumer, at the psychic expense of a multi-hued nation that would just like to get on with the 21st century. ✧

ART

POST ROAD

Nelson Bakerman

WILDWOOD

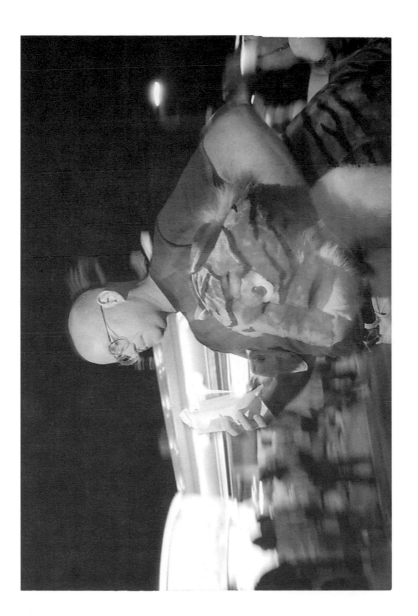

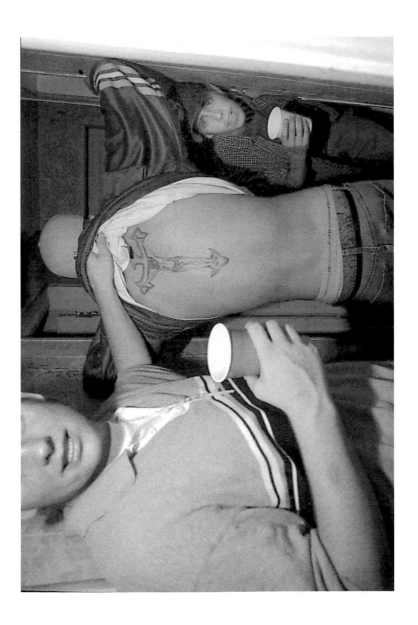

Nelson Bakerman

WILDWOOD

*

The photographs on pages 97 through 109 were selected from Nelson Bakerman's ongoing Wildwood series, which he began in the summer of 1996. The series focuses largely on the teenage pick-up scene along the boardwalk, and the other people who flock to this Jersey Shore amusement park. As a teenager Bakerman had his own penny arcade at Wildwood, and began his photographic career shooting in this same locale back in the late 1970s.

Woodward Gallery, located in the heart of
New York's SoHo art district, specializes in
developing private and corporate art
portfolios with the unique painting and
sculpture of their emerging and established
artists, and through contemporary masters from
Picasso to Warhol. Limited edition prints by
POP artists such as Indiana, Lichtenstein,
Raushenberg, and Warhol and a selection by
their Gallery stable are available as well.

Please visit our website at
http://www.artnet.com/woodward.html

WOODWARD
GALLERY

476 BROOME STREET, 5TH FLOOR, NEW YORK, NY, 10013-2281
(212) 966-3411 FAX (212) 966-3491 TUES. - SAT., 11 AM - 6 PM

www.artkrush.com

NONFICTION

POST ROAD

My Word: Memoir's Necessary Betrayal

Lee Martin

In the lobby of Burgin's Nursing Manor, where I've come to visit my cousin Roger, birdsong serenades us. It's early evening, dusk falling outside, and we sit by the glass-encased aviary where songbirds flit about among the silk greenery or poke their heads out of straw-colored nests to show off their brilliant colors: their yellows and oranges and reds, their greens and whites and blues. They warble and trill, and from time to time, Roger points and announces a particular bird's common name. There are specific species of canaries and doves, buntings and tanagers. I tell myself I'll remember the descriptive names, but I know I'll end up forgetting.

Roger, though, forgets very little. All his life, he's been able to learn, and to recall at will, not only the dates of family births, marriages, deaths, but also minutiae: the makes and years of cars people have driven, street addresses, appliance brands, the names of pets long gone. Even now, at age seventy-three, his memory is sharp.

So I've come to ask him about our grandfather, who died in 1941 when Roger was fifteen and my birth lay fourteen years in the future. I want to know what kind of man Will Martin was so I might better understand the tendency toward anger that runs through our family and that caused years of difficulty between my father and me.

"Do you remember our grandfather?" I ask.

Roger nods his head. "Oh, sure. I remember Grandpa. Will Martin had horses. He had Dolly and Dan and Prince and. . ." Roger rattles off more names than I can hold in my head, seemingly every name of every horse our grandfather ever owned.

I realize, with a tremendous disappointment, that when it comes to portraying the inner life—the essence of Will Martin that I crave—Roger is inept. He is armed only with facts. Like the birds, he could sing on and on. But whatever Will Martin was inside himself—however he affected those who knew him—will remain a secret, a blank left for me to fill through imagination and language.

I never knew my father with hands. One day in November 1956, when I was just over a year old, the shucking box on his corn picker jammed. A tooth on a roller had sheared off, and the roller couldn't feed the shelled corn on through the auger. He tried to clear the corn from the shucking box without first shutting down the power take-off, a risky thing for any farmer to do, and the picker's spinning rollers pulled in first one hand and then the other. By the time another farmer driving past the field heard his cries for help, my father's hands were so mangled that a surgeon had to amputate them.

Though there was a year when my father was able to hold me, now I can barely imagine it.

I knew more intimately the prostheses he wore on a harness of canvas straps that settled across his shoulders. Each morning, when my mother helped him dress, he slipped his stumps into flesh-colored plastic holsters. At the end of each holster was a set of two steel prongs curved like questions marks. These were the "hooks" that he used to grasp everything from a ballpoint pen to a drinking glass. Cables ran along the length of each holster to a lever and a layer of thick rubber bands at the base of each hook. He could open his hooks by contracting the muscles in his shoulders, tightening the cables that ran down to levers, pulling against the tension of the rubber bands, and spreading the prongs. One of the prongs was smooth on the inside; the other was gridded like a meat pounder. When he wasn't wearing them, I would often spread the hooks apart. I would slip my slender arms down into the holsters and try to figure out how everything worked.

My father was quick to anger, and when I was a child, he often whipped me with his belt. Later, when I was a rebellious teenager, our confrontations grew more violent, and he used his hooks against me as weapons. One night, he jabbed the point of a hook into my throat, and I feared that he might kill me. Through all our fights, and even after we had finally reached a reconciliation, I never talked to him about that moment in the cornfield or asked him anything about the accident or what it had been like for him. I was afraid. I didn't know how to invite him to talk about something so personal. I never felt I had the right.

It was only as I grew older and became, and then passed, the age my father was when the accident occurred that I began to understand that his story was mine, that whatever he had carried into our home when he had returned from the hospital, his hands gone forever—whatever anger, regret, rage—had become my future, a destiny it would take me years to understand and transcend.

Charles Baxter, in his essay, "Shame and Forgetting in the Information Age," calls attention to the number of recently published literary memoirs in which fathers or stepfathers distort family history thereby creating a dysfunctional narrative. The literary memoir, Baxter argues, is an antidote to this disfigurement.

The narrative of my own family was dysfunctional in the sense that there was no narrative, at least none about our single defining moment. My parents, nor any close relatives, ever spoke to me about my father's accident—no doubt the most significant episode of all our lives—and as a result, I became a spy, an observer, an interpreter, an inventor as I watched and listened closely for clues to why my father was so easily provoked to anger and why I rarely felt that he loved me enough. In some sense, then, I suppose I was always the writer, compelled to find words to fill the silence.

In 1996, when my collection of short stories, appeared, Amy Bloom, in her foreword, called attention to the fact that one of my aunts had been displeased with me for using some of the family stories in my work. This aunt, the wife of my mother's brother, had trusted me with these stories, and I had understood that I wasn't to retell them. But since none of my family members were readers of literary fiction, I felt confident that they would never see any of the stories that I published. Then a neighbor, on vacation in Vermont, picked up a journal in a bed and breakfast, saw one of my stories, and later told my aunt, who was "irked," as folks in my part of the country are apt to say when they're angry.

The people on the farms and in the small towns of southeastern Illinois spend lifetimes guarding their privacy while at the same time being eager for gossip about their neighbors. Like most people, they want a story; they just don't want to be the subject of the narrative. Even to see one's name in print or to hear it broadcast during the local news on the radio is usually not a desirable experience. Most often, the only experiences these people have with notoriety are at times of tragic loss (accident, illness, death) or shame (misdemeanors, felonies, divorces). Granted, there are times when a name, even a photograph, can appear in the local newspaper and be cause for celebration: births, weddings, anniversaries, employee of the month at the local Wal-Mart, 4-H Fair winner, grower of prize tomatoes or cucumbers. But even this publicity can evoke anxiety, as in the case of a woman I know who was recently tempted to take one of her glamorous tomatoes to the *Olney Daily Mail* office but decided against the idea because, as badly as she wanted to be photographed, she couldn't bear the thought of her face appearing in the paper. "I don't want anyone to know who I am," she said. "I don't want them to know where I live."

But she does want to know what goes on in other people's houses. She gossips about the divorcee who lives across the street and a certain gentleman's car seen there at three in the morning. "Isn't that terrible?" she says, anxious for someone to agree. In restaurants or grocery stores, she makes no effort to hide her astonishment at seeing someone she considers too thin, too fat, too underdressed, too overdressed, too. . .you fill in the blank. "Look at that," she'll say in a too-loud voice. "My word."

Her own privacy, though. . .ah, *that* is a different matter. "It's no one's business what I do," she says. She keeps her curtains closed, taping them down at the sides so there won't be the slightest gap where someone might be able to see in. She does her banking in a town twenty miles away so no one in Olney will know how much money she has. If she's in her house at night, all the doors and windows locked, and she wants to tell someone something private, she'll come close and whisper, just in case someone's lurking outside trying to eavesdrop.

I admit that she's an extreme example of a person fearing invasion into her private life but representative, nonetheless, of people like my aunt, who always refuses the local society correspondent calling for news of family visits, shopping trips, birthday celebrations, and who finally said to me after she realized I wasn't to be trusted, "I'm not going to tell you another thing. You'll put it in a book."

Patricia Hampl describes the act of writing memoir as a collision between memory and imagination. "The casualty," she says, "is the dead body of privacy lying smashed on the track." If my cousin Roger is the faithful guardian of facts, then I am the subversive, anxious to take these facts and use them to tell a story—my story—a narration heretofore hidden from me in my family's silence about my father's accident and its consequences.

I remember once at a Christmas gathering, when I was around ten, the excitement I felt when I learned that there was to be a showing of home movies. How grand, I thought. A cousin was setting up the screen, snapping reels onto the projector. I lived in a house where the few snapshots we took had to be taken with a borrowed camera. To see my relatives, maybe even myself at an earlier age, moving about on the screen was about the most delightful thing I could imagine. But before the show could get underway, one of my uncles pointed out to my cousin that my father would be in the movies—my father before his accident, when he still had his hands. "I don't think Lee should see that," my uncle said in a low voice he didn't mean for me to hear. But I did, and immediately I felt the excitement drain from the afternoon. I also felt a touch of shame, being the object of pity. I was aware of being outside the family by virtue of my father's circumstances, loved all the same, but not allowed to fully participate for fear some harm might come to me. I knew there would always be more to my father's story, and to mine, than anyone would be willing for me to know.

Now I would give up practically anything to see those movies, even to have seen them then, so I would have their images in my mind, images of my father and his hands. I imagine him in the slightly jerky frames of the film. Perhaps he's sitting at a kitchen table, snapping cards down with a flourish as he takes a trick in a game of pitch. I can see his gold wedding band catch the light and glint. After all the cards are played, he snaps his fingers and pops his palm against his fist, that timeless good-guy gesture that says everything's aces. Or maybe he's outside on a sunny afternoon, putting on some silly face for the camera. He's juggling three oranges. Then I'm there, crawling across the grass. He catches the oranges and stuffs them into his jacket pocket. Then he scoops me up in his hands, lifts me above his head, raises me toward the sky. Perhaps if I had watched those home movies, I would have seen that my father had once been a happier man. Maybe I would have understood that the accident had changed him, filled him with rage. Maybe something significant would have happened for both of us that afternoon. We might have learned to be more tolerant, to humble ourselves before the horrible things that could happen in a life to change it forever.

From the time of biblical parables, through Aesop's fables, to Grimm's fairy tales, and beyond, people have hungered for narrative, not only as entertainment or a record of events but also because it is through story that we understand. We come to know what it is to experience the world from someone else's perspective. We comprehend our own behaviors more fully. We learn that for each individual action there is a consequence. Through stories, we become more human.

When there is silence, no story being told, it is human nature to invent a narrative. The memoirist, working from memory and observation, gathering information from photographs, letters, newspaper reports, conversations, attempts to create a narrative that is as accurate and as truthful as it can possibly be. In some case, it may be more truthful than any distorted versions that might already exist. If the existing narrative, after all, were completely satisfying, what would be the need for the memoir?

We have long been aware that fiction, with its ability to reveal the hidden inner life, the one we mask with our own distorted narratives, gives us ourselves and our worlds in startling relief. Memoir attempts this as well but perhaps with a greater risk attached. The fiction writer works through the art of disguise, morphing actual people and experiences into created characters and events; the memoirist is, of course, more exposed, dealing as he or she does with actual people, sometimes still living, who may not take kindly to their appearance on the printed page. The essence of memoir as a genre is confession and revelation. Such exposure puts in danger the integration of the self, the memoirist, and his or her community, most often represented by family.

In my own case, it's not so much a question of offending family members by making them look bad. The only person in my memoir who is still alive to object to the character flaws I expose is me. My father has been gone seventeen years, my mother, eleven. My grandfather, Will Martin, about whom I speculate in connection with my father's life and my own, has been dead nearly sixty years. My grandmother, Stella, died in 1965.

I worry, though, that there are surviving family members who may object. After all, I'm airing the dirty laundry, most of it belonging to my father and me, but that very act may easily seem to some a betrayal. I'm afraid some family members may never be able to understand that the past belongs to none of us. It's simply story, mine to tell as much as it is theirs if they choose. My father lost his hands and became an angry man. For years, I lived a turbulent life with him. My mother, who despite her devout belief in goodness—or perhaps because of it—frequently bore silent witness to our violence. Those are facts, and if memoir is more than revenge—if it's indeed one writer's attempt to revisit the past in order to come to terms with it and then move on—how can he or she turn away from any piece of experience, even from other people's lives, that will enable the effort?

I realize that the writer has all the power in this situation: the power to decide what gets told and what doesn't, the power to name or not to name. In my own memoir, I've tried my best to protect the people who were accidental participants in my family's drama—the friends, neighbors, acquaintances with whose lives our own briefly intersected. Of course, I've changed their names. What's more, I've felt compelled to change the names of certain family members. I've even done it in this essay. Roger is an invented name for my cousin. There is one excerpt from the memoir, published in a small literary journal when I was still struggling with the question of what I owed my family in the way of privacy, in which I used Roger's real name. If anyone cared to find it, they could, but I don't suppose it matters much. I imagine anyone who knows my family will be able to read the memoir and figure out exactly who's who. Even though I may only be covering gashes with Band-Aids, it's the best I can do while writing what I had to in order to heal my own wounds.

For some reason, I decided to use the real names of my mother's family members, perhaps because they play a less crucial role in the family history or perhaps because I always thought of them as the more level-headed and human side of my family. I might have left them out altogether if not for the fact that they were sometimes necessary to my understanding of my mother and the roles she accepted and the ones she refused to play. Nowhere in the book do any of the living come off looking bad. Still, I've heard from a cousin on my mother's side of the family that there are other cousins who are cursing my name for revealing that our grandfather, my mother's father, was an alcoholic. It pains me to hear such news. Despite my need to tell my story, I believe in the fabric of family and have no desire to rend it.

The family members, now gone, about whom I write, were all good people, as are those who survive and their children. I can think of no one on my father's or my mother's side of the family who ever intended evil, not even my father with whom I fought so terribly, or me who made my own mistakes. Still we were, and are, flawed, and, if my task as a writer is to see clearly and fully, as it surely must be, I've had to reveal those flaws, my father's and my own most of all.

I suppose, in some sense, this is an apology to any of my family members, whether included in the memoir or not, who may read it and think me a traitor simply because I've dared to put myself, my father, my mother, my grandparents, my aunts and uncles on the page. All I can say is, I've tried to do it with respect and understanding of each of their stories and how they relate to my own. Patricia Hampl, in her book, *I Could Tell You Stories: Sojourns in the Land of Memory,* points out that, although many attack the memoir these days as an act of self-absorption, it is actually an attempt to discover not only the self but also to connect with the world outside the self. Indeed, if we are to know ourselves, we must transcend to a level of consciousness from where we can see the community in us and also us in the community. Opening ourselves to all experience, understanding that we all share in an individual story, is perhaps the wisest, most humane, most loving act we can perform.

On this day in the nursing home, I gently try to steer Roger to the information I'm seeking. "Was our grandfather anything like my dad?"

And that's when Roger gives me the one fact I never could have predicted, a detail that stuns me with its irony. "Oh, I reckon. Sure, I guess. One of his hands was sort of twisted." Roger spreads the fingers of his left hand and holds it, claw-like, on his knee. "Then your dad got his hands in that corn picker."

I want to stop him. I want to know why Will Martin's hand was deformed. I want to know why my father never spoke of it even though deep down I already know. I come from a family, so typical on the farms of southern Illinois where I grew up, that guarded its privacy generation by generation, that buried narrative along with its tragedies, that never could have imagined that I, the last one of them to come into the world, would one day tell everything I knew, everything I suspected. I'm sure they would think now, if they were still with me, that I had betrayed them.

Roger tells a story about our grandfather's horses, a story passed down to him. It was a few months after my father was born in 1913, and Will Martin and his brother-in-law, Dave Hill— "That was Ida's husband," Roger says. "Our Grandma Stella's sister. There was Idie and Stellie and Laurie and

Nellie and Fannie and the two boys, Elmer and Fred." He goes on to tell about Dave Hill and Will Martin each plowing with a team of horses one evening when a storm came up and lightening struck Dave Hill. "Grandpa came a tearing up the lane. Driving that team of horses. It was Dolly and Prince. The buckles on their harness were jingling to beat the band."

Suddenly, I'm not listening. I'm imagining that night when Dave Hill lay dead in the field and Will Martin drove his team of horses wildly up the lane, carrying the news. And later, when Dave Hill's body had been carried to the mortuary, and Ida had been comforted, and it was quiet in the house, the rainstorm now only a sound of wet leaves dripping, a scent of clean air, a chill on the wind, did Will Martin find himself bent over my father's cradle? It's the story I prefer. I imagine it now, give it words to make it so: my grandfather, thinking how lucky he is to be alive; my father, sleeping sweetly, absolved from all that's yet to come. Perhaps he even wakes, reaches out, and Will Martin touches him, amazed by how small each finger is, how perfect, how different from his own. I leave them there, Will Martin petting his son, touching him ever so shyly with his twisted hand, on this night when death has come and they have both survived.

When I was a child, I would sit in the Church of Christ and at the end of the service occasionally witness a member who had fallen astray go to the front of the congregation during the invitation call. Almost always, this man or woman would be weeping. Usually, their transgressions would already be well-known. When the singing stopped, the preacher always announced that a lost child had come home. I remember the feeling I had at those moments—such awe that the person had come forward to make their wrongs public, such admiration, such love for the weakness of people and the strength. I always felt a little sorry for them, too, having to stand there, faces shiny with tears, shoulders heaving with their sobs. Then the preacher would ask them whether they wished to rededicate their lives to Christ, and they would nod, and that would be enough to put an ache in my throat—that gentle movement, that yes.

"Yes," we all seemed to be saying after the service when we rushed to the ones who had been lost. We shook their hands. We hugged them to us. We welcomed them back to the fold, their coming forward—their confession—bringing us all closer because we knew we weren't so different, all of us vulnerable, imperfect, but together for the time, doing the best we could with our lives and the stories we couldn't stop them from telling. ✧

Moving Water

Kevin Holdsworth

Neighbors shouldn't be too good. How are you going to recompense all those home-cooked meals, plates of cookies, or every favor large or small? You can't. I'm not saying neighbors should be bad, either; it's just easier to deal with people in between. Plus, things change—people move or pass away. Too-good neighbors leave too-large gaps, as my first Torrey neighbor did.

Torrey, in scenic south-central Utah, is an edge community. Geographically, it lies on the edge of the earth: at once on the cusp of the Colorado Plateau and as the eastern doorstoop of the High Plateaus province. The town sits at 6850 feet, beneath and between two 11,000-foot mountains, with infernal red desert country falling away to the east, and nothing but trouble other directions. In the old days, Torrey was a last outpost: heading into the canyons, into Robbers Roost, or along the Outlaw Trail, it was the last toehold of civilization for a hundred wasteland miles. Morally, at least according to the oh-so-righteous up-county people, Torrey has always enjoyed a shady reputation: for moonshine and horse racing in the old days, for hippies in the '70s, and now for outsiders. Regarding religion, Torrey has for years been a town split in thirds, a rarity in southern Utah: one third faithful Latter Day Saints, one third backsliding or "Jack" Mormons, and one third irredeemables: Baptists, Catholics, pagans, witches, birdwatchers, vegetarians, Sierra Clubbers, and sundry other heathens. There stand churches of three different faiths in town—not bad considering 125 year-round residents. Scientists, too, look to an edge community for hardiness, for diversity, for the ability to adapt to harsh circumstances. My first neighbor was a survivor, a relict, a remnant of an earlier time.

Doug Wells grew up in Hanksville, Wayne County, Utah. His nephew, LaVar Wells, actually digs wells for a living out of that sandblasted town, where the Fremont River meets Muddy Creek and becomes the Dirty Devil. Doug himself dug wells, drove trucks, gathered firewood, punched cattle, a thousand other jobs in his time, but mainly what he wanted to do in his late fifties, when I knew him, was to raise a few cattle. Not because it made any economic sense. It didn't. But because that's what he knew. He shuttled his critters between Torrey and his home at the mouth of Weber Canyon, near Ogden. He also had a winter grazing allotment near Hite, in the Cheesebox-White Canyon country, but the road was so damned rough down there, the feed so scarce most years, the waterpockets just dried up, and the predators so brazen, that he usually penned and fed his cattle up north and brought them to Torrey from late spring to early fall.

Doug and I had an unspoken competition to see who could get up the earliest and work the hardest. Dawn would find him out in the pasture moving water, irrigating. On mornings, he'd repair some equipment or run errands. Afternoons, he spent making furniture or working on his cabin. Evenings, he'd find something to do—under floodlights if he had to. He beat me hands down, even with a three-decade head start.

There's something about this land that makes you overdo it—a toehold mentality. You gaze around yourself and see nothing but wilderness—wide-stretching mountains, sun-baked canyons and mesas, moony badlands—and you'd like to do your part to domesticate your little quarter. Also there is the problem of the weather, particularly the wind: five thousand feet of vertical relief makes for some full-on shaking and rattling. Faced with a raging world out of control, you want to batten down what you can after a three-day blow.

But Doug Wells was more than just a maniac rancher; it doesn't take any élan to work hard. He was also an artist cowboy. He wrote good cowboy poetry. At the end of the day, when the work was done, he liked nothing better than to set on his back porch, abuse a guitar, and sing to his cattle. Sometimes the critters were gentled by his song. Other times they milled restlessly and probably begrudged his high-pitched coyote wail. When he warbled "Red River Valley," let me tell you, he meant it.
"Won't you sit by my side if you love me,
Do not hasten to bid me adieu—"
I've never seen anyone irrigate with such determination, as if he took the dry spells personally. Water is blood to a desert cowboy. When the ditch water was flowing onto his land, he wouldn't let it pool up, coagulate too long. Nothing much to it, he'd say: put on your boots, get down into your work, and keep it moving. Six days on the ditch, six days off—just enough to transfuse fifty acres of pasture. He irrigated during snowstorms, during the rain. I believe he went out there at night: checking headgates, fixing dams.

You know how sometimes people resemble their dogs or vice versa? With Doug, it was horses. He owned one very stuck-up open mare that wouldn't even give you the time of day when her owner was around. But one time, when he was away, I went over to give Miss Hoity-Toity an apple. It was spooky: she had the same wrinkles over the eyes, the same bulldog neck, the same perpetual sunburn, the same sly grin, even the same laconic manner as Doug.

We talked about the water level in the ditch, about the weather. Doug was a master of dry understatement. After I built a seven-foot-high windbreak fence, he said, "Guess your horse won't be jumping over that one." Or when he asked me to watch his horses while he was away, "If that old gelding don't move for two or three days, you might wanna call the vet." Or after a three-day grit storm, "Gee, don't the air smell fresh this morning?" Or when I managed to get my truck stuck in an irrigation ditch, "You probably don't want to just *leave* your outfit there for too long. Winter's coming... How 'bout I give you a little tug out?"

There was a more contentious side to our relationship, though. One time in May, Doug and I were cleaning out the ditch before it opened. We were both down in the clayey bottom of the main stem, grubbing around in the mud and roots. Maybe it was the feel of the shovel, or the weight of the sod, but the struggle—and it was the same old seasonal struggle: there's never *enough* water, and those downstream people in Hanksville have a prior right, so just when you need it most, in August, they get more than their share of it, and the damned spider-rooted sod always seems to grow, tangled up and hard to pull out, recalcitrant as children or a bad dog—the struggle must have set him off.

"Them damned environmentals," he said, apropos of agriculture, "they're against *everything* human. Hell, where do you think *food* comes from? They sure don't grow it at the supermarket."

I didn't look his way. Sometimes Doug would doff his sombrero and reveal the whitest forehead you've ever seen. His face was like some of the cliffs: red on bottom, white above, and barren on top. I knew Doug was baiting me. We were a couple of bull elk in September. I studied the vegetation.

"Nature," he said. "I'll teach you something about nature. Hell, I'm just as much a lover of nature as any of them damned environmentals."

"Sure, Doug. No doubt about it."

People can take things personally if they want.

The fact was the local water conservancy district, duped by a slick civil engineer from Spanish Fork, had big plans to build a cash-register dam one mile above town. This dam might well have provided *beaucoup* water to Doug and the four or five other ranchers on Poverty Flat, but the project had many problems, mainly economic and ecological, and I had been active in the dam's opposition, organizing a local anti-dam "committee."

It was only natural for Doug to want to *improve* nature. That a reservoir full of water—impounded, stored, and used—would be an improvement, could not have been more obvious. Moreover, you grow up in Hanksville, as Doug had, and doing virtually anything seems an improvement: shoveling sand from your driveway, gathering coal out on Factory Bench, hauling an old wreck off the place, dating someone who is not your cousin, making coffee. Improvements all. A dam was easy.

I wanted to explain how the dam would end up costing way more than the dreamy predictions of the civil engineer, that the engineer had deliberately played fast and loose with the facts, that cash-register dams never pay for themselves, that the reservoir basin would be an ugly mud flat most of the year, that constructing a power plant 800 feet from the border of a National Park was a terrible idea, and so on, but I held my tongue.

"You bet, Doug."

"And now them crooked politicians are starting to sound like environmentals too... They sure couldn't make it any harder on us."

"No question about that. What does all that money go for anyway? It sure isn't helping us any."

The shovels went down easy enough, but the sod was heavy and entwined, hard on your back. We kept at it for another hour in silence, except for grunting and occasional low curses. Maybe we taught each other a lesson.

Pretty as Doug Well's pasture was, it proved easy living to just sit outside and watch the cows and calves float along late in the day, legs half lost in timothy and wire grass. Or see how his Hereford-Angus cross Range Bull would call the ladies and kids over for a noontime lesson. Who cared about a few flies? Better cows than condos. Someday someone will carve up the pasture into a few choice ranchettes, but if you remember things the way they were before, you keep the image with you.

Sure, there was a flip side to it, and it came in late October and early November, or after calving time. I like beef—broiled, grilled, basted, roasted, pan fried, barbecued—and find it hard to imagine any western American cow as holy. The selling and slaughter is what pays the bills. Still, certain times of year brought on the distraught cries of the mothers, and insofar as the little ones knew, they knew that the gambols of summer, the games of chase and buck, the taste of ditch water and good deep grass were over. The life of a cow leads only to Salina, and thence to the Killing Floor. May is a poor time not to have a calf at your side, and November is a deadly time to be a bull calf.

In the end, though, it didn't pay for Doug. He had to sell the place to help pay medical bills for his stepdaughter. His duty demanded it, and he sold the ranch to a hobby cowboy who rode a four-wheeler and didn't even own a decent horse. The new neighbor, aside from his fondness for the internal combustion engine (he once had his tractor, truck, four-wheeler, generator, air compressor and chainsaw all going at the same time) proved to be a gentleman, even if he wore a baseball cap and went to church every Sunday. He never gave me the slightest reason to soil his memory. He sold out four years later.

More recently, the pasture was leased by Mr. J., a shithead from nearby Bicknell, who, in addition to cutting my fence, breaking a gate, digging up the bridge into my place that had stood for fifty years, letting his cattle graze in my field *because the alfalfa was there and I wasn't,* and then attempting to deny all of the above to my then-pregnant wife (not a good idea, to be sure) when the evidence was perfectly clear, Mr. J. then proceeded to explain how the problem was *you newcomers, people that come in here and try to tell us old-timers what to do with our land.* He said he just wanted to be a good neighbor, but he wasn't sure he'd be able to now. Excuse me! My wife pointed out the land in question was *ours, not his,* and that it would be a very good idea for him to leave and that presently. I told him I would call the sheriff. Oh yes, Mr. J. made a person nostalgic for the old days.

Years later, after I moved and was living in Ogden, while driving on Highway 89, the freeway they built through his front yard in South Weber, I saw Doug. I couldn't bring myself to stop. He had clearly aged, and I wanted to fix him in time, like a monarch butterfly, the kind that migrate through Torrey and feed only on milkweed, because there was so much of him that was both timeless and already vanishing.

Still, I imagine I see him occasionally, steering his old blue Ford tractor around the pasture, spreading fertilizer pellets in light-falling late-March snow. ✧

Shouting Obscenities at George Bush the Younger

Olisa Corcoran

I joined the freak show. I was a freak. I paid bus fare to do it. It was great.

Erin—a tall, aloof woman who never shares her political views with me—instigated it. We were in a bar. We were drinking vodka. Erin said she wanted to do something, she didn't know what, just *something*, about this Bush inauguration. "It's a *coup d'etat*. I want to do something."

A *coup*... I had heard it said of the Bush victory before, but I was overcome by the sting of the characterization. I'm not sure whether anger or a thirst for excitement held the greater sway, but when Erin suggested we join the inauguration protest, I assented. Avidly. As long as she made the arrangements.

So Erin dug around on the Internet and found us a Washington D.C.-bound bus to join. It was a group of lawyers very angry about voting irregularities, a fairly mainstream group of middle-aged people with teenaged kids, who baked cookies for the four-hour trip from North Carolina. We slept on the bus. I had to wake at 3:45 a.m. to catch it, an irrational hour that nearly prevented me from participating. The organizers passed around Sharpie pens to write the telephone number of a legal aid group on our arms, in case we got arrested.

My first major creep-out of the day happened on that bus when the lawyers started to kvetch about Bush. "He got off on his military service. The rest of us had to serve, but he got special treatment." "He's a slippery bastard." "He is so arrogant." "I hate his smug grin." "He is going to mess this country up. Bad."

I realized that it was early and that might explain the atrophied level of discourse. But I had the disturbing feeling that these attorneys were simply repeating the same hackneyed phrases that busloads of Republicans must have leveled at Bill Clinton on the way to various weirdo right-wing rallies over the last eight years. Simply replace angry middle-aged men in cowboy hats and polo shirts with angry middle-aged men with beards and the occasional earring. And I was among them. I covered my head with my blanket and tried to sleep.

When we arrived in Washington—or rather the Metro station in suburban Virginia—Erin and I both pulled out our compacts, checked our eyeliner, and applied lipstick. Everyone gathered their protest signs and climbed off the bus, facing regular people, non-protesters, face-to-face for the first time. I was startled by Erin's homemade poster: "Hail to the Thief." During the course of the day we'd see many people with the same poster—some organization even printed them en masse—but at that point, sober and far from home, I looked at Erin with a new fear.

My own poster said "Fuzzy Vote Count, Fuzzy Presidency," on one side and "No Mandate" on the other. Fairly non-threatening, I thought. But my husband Rick made the sign for me, and it was in his strange, italic block lettering, which is unlike the handwriting of anyone else I know—an intense, slanting penmanship that made the mildness of the sentiment fierce, like some kind of staff festooned with wolf fangs.

"Cool poster, Olisa," someone said to me. I panicked. How the hell did she know my name? I remembered the nametags the organizers had distributed, and I quickly ripped mine from my chest.

It was cold, drizzly, and gray. We stood around the bus waiting for signs to be distributed to protesters who'd come unarmed. One woman excitedly took a large foam board with "D.U.I.—Dubbya's Undeserved Inauguration" from the leader of our bus. People clapped when they read that one. I laughed nervously.

We walked together through the crowded train station, a sort of mini protest march. Assorted groups of protesters from other buses milled about, but otherwise the platform belonged to the unaffiliated or to the Bush supporters who were going into the city to watch the inaugural parade. I don't even like political bumper stickers, and here I was, stirring up trouble in the metro. I stood close to the woman with a sign reading *"Attencion Presse Etranger! Bush est un voleur!"* and hoped that the people around me didn't read French.

At one point I put my arm around Erin and leaned close. "We're one of the crazies, Erin," I whispered. She laughed it off. I kind of meant it, but I was afraid to tell her.

What happened between those early moments of discomfort and my transformation an hour later into a woman who actually screamed *"Muerte a Bush!"* into a Univision camera, I can't say for sure. The thousands of protesters massed in Dupont Circle with signs ranging from "Ave Scalia—The Immaculate Selection" to "Bush + Dick = Screwed!" had something to do with it. The clumps of Republican women wearing their furs on the Metro and scowling at us certainly helped. Cops in riot gear. The intense pleasure of being surrounded by people who also rode in buses to protest the inauguration. The chanting. The marching. The shouting.

Erin and I quickly joined the group from Justice Action Movement marching down to the parade route. We saw a group of nervous-looking people with mysterious beige sock puppets on their hands marching beside us. A particularly shrill young woman led us in a chant of "What do we want? Democracy! When do we want it? Now!" Passing cars tooted their horns in support. I noticed a tight-skinned, alarmingly pale man swerving as he walked alongside me, without a poster, sipping from a tiny pewter flask. Folks in the houses along the streets cheered and took our photos. We chanted exuberantly, "We own the streets! The streets are ours!" That's when I saw the Univision crew. I couldn't pass up the opportunity to say something wild and inflammatory in a foreign language, but my Spanish escaped me, and all I came up with was the simpleminded "Death to Bush!"

Once I shouted that, I was free to really let go.

Erin was a great protester, shouting all of the chants, waving her "Hail to the Thief" sign around. It was an unreserved, wild Erin—very different from the glamorous, ironic woman I knew back home. We shouted "Racist, Sexist, Anti-Gay! Bush and Cheney, Go Away!" I didn't even feel all that uncomfortable about it, although now I'm a little freaked out that I actually said such a thing. Shouted such a thing, no less. We walked past a Whole Foods supermarket, and a woman next to me suddenly said, "Oh look, a Whole Foods. I love that store." I thought, don't you feel all of the crazy energy around us? Whole Foods, for Godsake?! This is democracy, baby. Who cares about fucking Whole Foods?!

The first leg of our march bottled up at 14th and K streets, across from Franklin Square, which turned out to be one of the only places arrests were made and protesters bloodied. Suddenly, the march stopped, and we were mildly pushed from behind by other protesters.

That's when the helicopters began circling. That's where the police buses were lined up to haul off protesters. That's where I saw a man in a sports coat urging us to "Push forward" against the barricades and the line of cops in riot gear. A wild-faced man was pushed along in his wheelchair by a man in a Nixon mask. I thought they were going for a wacked-out terrorist look. There were a lot of people with ski masks and bandanas over their mouths. Erin said, "Let's move to the side." I quieted down and followed her.

The cops weren't going to let us through the blockade, which was angering a lot of the people around me. "We own the streets!" they shouted. I watched them shove each other. I didn't get it. Why were we marched down to a police barricade? I thought we had permits to march. I could see other protesters in the square across K Street, lots of young people in black with black flags shouting, "Let our brothers through!" They were the anarchists, the Black Block.

Erin and I left the clutch of people pushing against the police barricade and joined a group of stray protesters cutting through an alley between two high rises. Police choppers hovered over us in the crack of gray sky. I took that opportunity to call Rick on my cell phone. "Listen to the helicopters," I said and held up the phone to the air.

Without intending to, Erin and I wound up in Franklin Square, among the anarchists, looking back across K Street to the protesters we'd just left, who were shouting to the police to let them through. The Franklin Square crowd was early 20ish, with lots of dyed-neon hair and gas masks. A few tried to push their way past the cops into the street, only to be beaten down by billy clubs and swarmed by cameras. There were tentative little surges here and there. A couple ragtag young people in fatigues and latex gloves posed as "street medics." A pink-haired Asian girl shouted into a cell phone, "The cops are putting on their riot gear!" "But not their face masks," her buddy clarified, and she repeated into the phone, "Not their face masks. Not yet, anyway!"

Then a smallish young man in tight black clothes and a helmet appeared before us. He shimmied up the lightpole and stood on a metal traffic box, about fifteen feet above our heads. We cheered like crazy when he pulled out a black flag and unfurled it in the rain. I was jumping up and down, even though I had no idea what the black flag signified. Someone handed him a small American flag, which, after period of struggling with his lighter in the drizzle—during which someone shouted, "Get that man a Zippo!"—he eventually managed to set afire. The tiny anarchist, as I came to think of him, waved the burning flag. The crowd on both sides of the streets went wild.

It was the first time I've ever seen someone burn a flag before my eyes, and its effect on me was a strange and overwhelming patriotism. I wanted to burn a flag, too! I thought, what a great country we live in where we can burn flags on Inauguration Day! Flag burning is freedom!

But then I felt myself get caught up in the little surges of protesters against the line of police. In front of us, a young dreadlocked man appeared to be attacked by a cop. Erin and I and a group of people around us moved away from the pushing and shoving. One of the tiny anarchists turned to us and angrily shouted, "Stand your ground!" As appealing as that sentiment was, I didn't quite understand what we were standing our ground against. I didn't see the value of getting into a battle with the cops so that the protesters on the other side could cross a street that was clearly barricaded. It seemed like a stupid thing to fight for. And although I couldn't articulate why I came to D.C., I knew it wasn't to fight the cops for the right to cross K Street.

I became angry with myself for being so riled up and not knowing what to do or why I was even in D.C. This rage was power, dammit. But it's not like I wanted to overthrow the government or anything as mob-rulish as that. But I didn't want to squander it either. I wanted to do something with it. I turned to Erin, "What should we do now?"

"Let's keep going. Let's find the parade," she said as she extinguished her cigarette with her boot.

And then it came to me. I wanted to get to the parade route. I wanted to see Bush himself and shout obscenities at him.

Erin and I drifted away from the anarchists at Franklin Square and joined up with another group of marchers winding its way to Pennsylvania Avenue. En route, she and I stopped to buy "Bush Cheated" buttons from a street vendor and to visit a long line of Port-A-Potties that were set up for Lord knows whom.

The temperature dropped dramatically. Our chants became less energetic. Erin shouted, "We own the streets!" and I replied, "The streets are ours!" No one joined me in the chant, so the next time around I said, "The streets are mine."

The march petered out on the parade route, across from the National Archives. There, protesters mixed in with the mass of Bush supporters along the bleachers, and thus began a blurry three-hour period of rain and shivering while the divergent groups tried to ignore each other.

Erin and I climbed onto a perch on the statue in Market Square behind the bleachers. There were families of Bush supporters carrying little blue "Renewing the Spirit of America" placards. Lots of wet fur coats. Men in ties. But despite the fact we were on the official parade route, there seemed to be more protesters around than supporters.

A solo skinny man walked back and front of us carrying a "Bush Hates Fags" sign. Groups of young, attractive women in tight black clothes and silver pom-poms performed saucy, anti-capitalist cheers. And although I liked the content of their cheers, their scanty clothes and overall cuteness and the pleasure on the faces of the men watching them reminded me too much of actual high school cheerleaders, and it disturbed me. Only ugly, fat girls, or possibly homely men in drag, could have pulled that off with any semblance of real rebellion.

Any time a bus or police car went down Pennsylvania Avenue, we all booed. I have to admit that I'd no idea who was in the various vehicles that passed us, but I still booed. Erin and I stood shivering under our umbrellas. My sign had melted in the rain, and I wanted to ditch it, but I was afraid of looking like a Bush supporter, so I kept juggling it with my umbrella. I asked Erin if she knew when the parade would be passing by. "No idea," she said. I was weak from the cold.

I decided to check the messages on my cell phone. My mother had called, so I called her back. My dad answered and sounded nervous. "How's it going?"

I could hear the TV blaring in the background. I pictured him sipping a cabernet while stretched out on the overstuffed white sofa, flipping back and forth between myriad satellite channels' identical coverage of the inauguration.

"It's really freezing."

"We saw some protesters burning flags on TV. Are you with them?"

"I don't know if I was with them, but I was there, yes."

"It looked like it was pretty violent."

"Not at all. Just a little shoving."

"It looked like the police arrested some people."

"Really? By any chance, did they say on TV when the parade would be happening?"

"I don't know. Talk to your mother."

Mom came on, sounding choked up. "The inauguration ceremony was beautiful! Bush cried, his father cried. How's it going, honey?"

"Fine. Do you know what time the parade is supposed to happen? It's so damn cold."

"No, honey."

I called Rick and asked him, but he didn't know either.

Did I mention that it was bitter cold and raining? Bleak hours passed, during which Erin and I were mostly silent. A woman in a cow costume walked by with her dog, and a man with a Texas flag said, "I love animals." She smiled at him. "They taste great!" he shouted. "Lots of protein!"

At some point, I commented that there were people, sports fans, who sat in this bitter weather every weekend to watch football, the fools. It was the first thing I said in maybe an hour. Erin looked at me like I was making no sense, like she had never heard of such a thing. "You know, can't you picture those guys with giant chunks of fake cheese on their heads cheering in bleachers," I rambled. "It happens in this very country. Somewhere in the middle, I think."

She looked unconvinced.

In front of the bleachers across Pennsylvania Avenue, a thin woman walked by naked, except for a People for the Ethical Treatment of Animals placard. I thought of comparing her to the topless, barrel-bellied football fans I'd seen on TV but decided not to risk it again with Erin. Cops swooped up the PETA woman.

I began to convulse, and I leaned against Erin for warmth. She was stiff, and I felt rejected. "For a West Coast person, you're not very clingy," I said.

Erin looked genuinely taken aback. "I'm not very *clean?*"

"No, not clean. Clingy." I laughed nervously. "You know how West Coast people are all huggy and stuff compared to East Coast people?" I felt like an idiot. She just kind of stared at me. I was failing her as a protester. I was starting to whine. "I think I need to walk around a little. I'll be right back."

I ditched my ruined sign in a garbage heap and acquired a new one from some National Organization of Women volunteers. "No 'W!'" it read. I bought an "America, You've Been Bushwhacked!" T-shirt for Rick and watched a NOW activist walk up to a woman in a fur coat and say, "You know, he was selected, not elected."

"Four counts is enough for me, baby!" the mink-enshrouded woman shot back. Depressed by her energy and self-satisfaction, I kind of had to give that one to the Bush supporter.

I revived after purchasing hot cocoa from elegantly dressed men operating giant silver tureens, generous men with accents who said to every customer, regardless of top hats or dreadlocks, "Here is your coffee monsieur/madame." I joined Erin on our stoop. The cocoa dethawed me, and Erin and I started chatting again while she smoked.

Things picked up when, at the Navy Memorial on the corner, several tiny anarchists dressed in tight black clothes scaled a lightpost bedecked with flags, directly on the parade route. They pulled down the flags, and we protesters cheered, all of us, the Mumia people, the anti-fur people, the pro-choice people, the lawyers, the grandmothers from Florida—you name it. The Bush supporters seemed surprisingly quiet, but perhaps we just couldn't hear them over our hollers.

The nimble anarchists then somehow managed to hoist several black flags on the pole. I thought it was a beautiful victory for the protesters, in general, because they had actually managed to damage the parade route itself. I couldn't stop screaming. My judgement was impaired, and I actually joined a chant of "You suck! We hate you! We can't wait to replace you!" It was fabulous! I felt like I was really sticking it Bush and his irritating plea for a return to civility.

A row of riot cops ran in formation down the parade route. We viciously booed them. I heard one Bush supporter shout, "You get them boys!" The cops pulled down the black flags. The Republicans cheered.

Finally, the parade began. A group of military men with bayonets marched by. Predictably, we booed. A red-clad marching band came along. I felt sorry for them, but not sorry enough not to boo them. We booed at whoever came down the streets.

A limousine rolled along. This was our chance to be heard! Thinking it was Bush, the crowd went wild. "Shame!" they shouted. Obscenities came flying over my head. "You suck!" one woman shouted to Bush. "You are a shithead!" "I fucking hate you!"

As thrilled as I was to be exercising my rights to freedom of speech, I couldn't bring myself to shout, "Shame!" I laughed at the young Republican woman who turned to a disheveled protester and shouted, "Shave!"

Suddenly an arm emerged from the limo and waved. I focused on the crisp white French cuff and let out a deep wolf howl. "Fuck you!" the people shouted. People were giving the cuff the middle finger. People would have ripped off that haughty white cuff, if given the chance.

When I watched a videotape of the parade the next day, I couldn't figure whom the cuff belonged to. We may have been booing Clinton or Gore, for all we knew. It didn't matter to us.

Then two trucks with TV cameras and still photographers came along the route, and we all went wild again. Another chance to speak out! I wanted the world to see us dissing the inaugural parade. I lifted my sign as high as possible.

Just when I thought I couldn't scream more, the presidential limo appeared. You couldn't mistake it with the flags and Secret Service men running alongside. The crowds exploded into a fever of "Shame!" "Fuck You!" "You Suck!" "Fascist!" "Thief" "Illegitimate!" "Boo!!!" "I Hate You!" I didn't hear a single cheer.

The only time I've ever shouted louder was during a tornado when the roof was torn off my bedroom and I was thrown on the floor.

At least one Bush supporter was overcome by the howling and turned to the protesters with tears in his eyes. "Thanks for saying 'fascist!'" he cried. "That's great! Now I know what kind of idiots I'm dealing with."

"Fuck you!" I heard myself scream.

Unlike presidents in past inaugural parades, Bush the Younger didn't get out of his car until he was well past us and near the White House grounds, so it was at his car that we focused our anger. We saw the parade stop, and I later learned that it was because they felt security was threatened by protesters a little further along the route. He was smart not to get out of his car. I doubt anyone could take the fury and profanity we hurled at him.

We were a pissed-off group of people, and there were thousands of us. I didn't even realize how pissed off I was until I got there.

After Bush passed, more soldiers marched by. We booed them, but with less energy than the earlier military troops. For the first time, I could hear the Bush supporters cheering over the protesters.

Then a platoon of mounted policemen rode by on their horses. "Look at the horses!" the protesters shouted. A kind of levity come over the crowd. "Horsies!" screamed a young man who'd been saying "Fuck the Thief!" moments earlier. I could see the Bush supporters on the other side cheering the horses, too.

"See, we all agree that horses are good," I said to Erin, laughing, feeling pleased with my observation and with the release of tension.

But, thank God, Erin, in her wisdom, didn't bite. She simply frowned at me and shouted, "Free the Horses!" thrusting her "Hail to the Thief" sign in the air. "Free the Horses!"

I shouted with her. Several people joined us. "Free the Horses!" I fantasized about the horses tossing the cops off their backs and charging the Bush supporters on the bleachers. I envisioned blood splattering under their angry hooves. I wasn't going to be placated by the universal appeal of animals, dammit. Horses or not, I was still mad.

After the exhilaration of shouting profanities at the President on his inauguration day and swearing at cops and booing soldiers and cheering tiny anarchists as they burned American flags, it's hard to come back. On the packed Metro heading toward our bus, Erin and I were the only protesters in a sea of Bush supporters. I made it a point to be courteous, saying, "After you, sir," when I arrived at a turnstile at the same time as a well-dressed man with the hairdo of an anchorman. Clearly suppressing his rage for us spoilers, and bloated with Bush's call for a return to civility, the man did not want to appear less gracious than I. He stabbed the air with his index finger and said, "No miss, after you." Fuck you, I thought, and passed in front of him.

How can anyone stand to be one of *them?* I loved them and felt sorry for them. I wanted to say, Wasn't that amazing? Aren't we lucky to be Americans, you clueless bastards? I think I was smiling at them, but I may have been baring my teeth.

How am I going to behave myself on this train? I wanted to burn a flag, badly. Would I ever be able to explain how flag burning made me feel patriotic?

I wondered how Erin was holding it together so well. She had reverted to her placid self.

A Texan with a Bush sticker on his lapel shouted to his buddy to give him a camera. "I want to take a picture of these girls' buttons," he said. Only after he pointed the camera at our chests and our "Bush Cheated" buttons did he deign to speak to us. "I'm sure you girls don't mind."

"Not at all," replied Erin, smiling. "Pass the word." ✧

ETCETERA | POST ROAD

```
1023—NTC—Sampson—5-9-44—50M—A-37
                              Date Sept 12, 1944

              I have arrived at the Naval Training Center.

My address is:

                         Francis Arthur Flynn SS.

        Company No.  263      D-10 U
              U. S. NAVAL TRAINING CENTER
                    Sampson, New York

    (Do not use nickname)
```

(Graphical aid provided by Kirk Flynn.)

Letters Home from the Pacific, 1944-46, Francis Arthur Flynn [1]

Compiled and Edited by Rick Moody

September 1944

Dear Mother, Dad, and Peggy,

Well after being here two days I can only say that if the whole course is this easy it'll be a snap. However I don't expect it will be. Although what we've been doing (physical, shots, clothing issue, rudimentary drill and exercise and cleaning up and putting our clothes away) hasn't been hard it has taken most of our time. We will be here twelve weeks but there are a lot of rumors that differ with that, however, I'm inclined to think we'll be here that long unless some drastic change is made. The fellows here are "hail fellows well met," good guys and all that but the average is not very intelligent or filled with common sense. However, they're likeable and good natured. The names for a new boot are "skin head," "barber bait," "needle bait," and just plain "boot." We get quite a ribbing from the "old salts" who've been here all of two to ten weeks.

If I can keep my mouth shut [2] and pay attention to what's said and the rules I think I'll get along pretty well here.

They've got something new for me to do so I'll have to sign off. Write soon and often.

Love,
Jack ("Boot")

---

[1] *The author is my uncle, Jack Flynn, and his unenviable location, as indicated in the postcard, is basic training in upstate New York, toward the end of WWII. He wrote more than a hundred letters home during military service, from which these are excerpted. Despite his worldliness, Jack had just celebrated his eighteenth birthday. Most of his boarding-school classmates enlisted immediately upon graduation, as he did.*

Other pertinent facts: Jack hailed from the affluent suburbs of Westchester County; the "Peggy" mentioned in these letters is my mom, Margaret Maureen Flynn, ten years Jack's junior. Many of his letters were to her, and most of these were advisorial as to the necessity of swimming lessons and studying hard, etc. The New York Daily News is the newspaper that is mentioned here occasionally. My grandfather was to become publisher imminently. A post he held for some twenty-five years. Further notes are appended below.

[2] *Not an unusual sentiment from my uncle. Even by his own account, he was often a difficult person to get along with, given to provocation and argument.*

*

Sept. 19, 1944

Dear Mom & Dad,

    I thought I'd write and give you an idea of what we do on an average day. At five-thirty we arise and wash then fallout for exercises. Upon returning from this restful phase we move to cleaning up the barracks and our personal gear and lockers. We then trip lightly to chow. After partaking of the delicious food (bah!) we return to stand colors. We then proceed to classes which include instruction in all kinds of things. After another fine meal we turn to the physical side of things. This includes physical training, drill, obstacle course, and test in physical abilities. From four-thirty till nine-thirty when we go to bed is free time with the exception of chow and any special musters which may come up. In this period we clean up the barracks again, wash our clothes and ourselves. As I told Peggy the work here isn't hard it's just constant. In general this experience is funny. The fellows here are on the dull thick side and it is a case of the blind leading the blind. They're just like sheep. One, who by the way knows nothing whatsoever about the subject in question, makes a statement and they just follow. They seem to have no common sense but they're all good boys at heart. I've found a few fellows with whom I can talk and seem to have a little intelligence, however, outside of them, I shut up and stay shut.

    I received the newspaper[3] for the past three days and I want to thank you a lot it's just like a touch of civilization and home. If you can find anyone with nothing to do ask them to write me, we live for mail up here.

    My cold is practically gone and it hasn't bothered me a bit since I've been here.

    Please don't become upset if I don't write very often or very long letters, they keep us busy. I had to write this in shifts. No kidding mail means everything up here so please write often and get some other people to do the same.

Love to all,
Jack

---

3 *The Daily News.*

*

5 Oct. 1944

Dear Parents,

In the past few days we've been getting training in antiaircraft fire-tracer fire, dry land boat drill, lookout-day & night, twenty millimeter anti-aircraft gun practice, sound power phones, ship recognition, aircraft recognition and as usual drill, physical training and obstacle course. Been a busy little beaver haven't I?

The antiaircraft tracer fire is taught with a machine which is a secret but I can tell you that it's done with perspective glasses and motion pictures and electric eye rays.

Dryland boat drill is just to acquaint us with terms and orders so that when we practice in actual boats we'll know what to do.

Lookout trainer is very interesting[.] [W]e learn how to look for ships and planes at night as well as in the daytime. In this they have a room with a dimly lighted horizon in which ships move. We are required to state its relative bearing to the supposed ship we are on. Before all this begins we sit watching an instructional movie with red "Dark Adaptation" glasses on. These glasses adapt our eyes to the darkness and then we are able to see the ships (models) that are on the horizon. It was very interesting and instructional.

The 20 m.m. gun practice and sound-power phones were given us together. We learned how to fire, change barrels, and secure the gun. The sound power phones are really a great invention. They generate their own power by impulses given to them from your own voice – really amazing.

I guess I mentioned that I'm an A.P.O.: apprentice petty officer, that is I'm a platoon leader and get to wear undersize stripes of a second class petty officer while I'm in boot. I've had this position for about two weeks but I didn't want to tell you about until I was sure I'd keep it.

I may get a boot instructor's rate in swimming but that's not at all definite yet.

Well must close as the hour is late – 9:00 p.m. – Write often

Love,
Jack

United States Naval Training
Bainbridge, Maryland
[undated]

Dear Parents,

Back again at the old grind and it's as dull as ever, some day I join the Navy, but not at these training centers that's assured.

I'm sorry about the little altercation we had about my mode of dress but I guess we don't see the thing in the same light. In the future I'll attempt to conform with your desires on the subject.

I want you both to understand that I really appreciate all the marvelous things you've given me and done for me while on liberty. I understand that you've been doing things all for me and as callous and indifferent as I may seem at times I'm very grateful to you.

It would seem that your young son is continually in slight jams down here. Because I go to the movies fifteen minutes before the scheduled time and various other petty things, but so far nothing serious and I can guarantee you the little stuff will cease and there never will be anything serious.

I'm definitely serious about RT's[4] and I would like to make it. I don't know whether I can or not but I'm going to try. Next week sometime I think I'll have an opportunity to volunteer.

The weather here is marvelous and if it continues, and I can find time, I may be able to acquire a slight tan. Give my love to Peg and write soon.

Much love to all,
Jack.

*

18 Dec. '44

Dear Family,

Well your son won't be home for Christmas this year and it won't be the last time we might as well get used to it. This is pretty definite unless you

---

[4] *Radio technicians.*

know anyone who could pull some strings[5] and yank me out [or] some minor miracle occurs. I think that I will be home for New Year's, as a matter of fact I'm sure I will be, unless I get Christmas. Everyone on the center gets one or the other. I'd rather you didn't send me anything or try to call me, for one thing I'll be busy (I'm working in the mess hall now) for another I'd rather have a repeat Christmas or New Year's if that's okay with you.

Working in the mess hall is long, tiring, and very boring work but it's not hard or unbearable. We'll be here for two or perhaps three weeks[.] I think, however it will be only two.

It's snowing now but it's a warm, lazy, light snow, not at all like Sampson.

Please have Christmas this year just the same as it's always been.[6] I won't be there but the thought that it's unchanged and still going on means a very great deal to me. I don't want you to save it till New Year's either, I just want a little repeater then. Have a merry Christmas and expect me New Year's

Season's greetings and love to all,
Jack

*

20, Feb. '45

Dear Mom and Dad,

Well, little sonny-boy is in the hospital with Scarlet Fever but don't get excited. I'm getting better care than I ever expected from the Navy. I'm in a marvelously comfortable bed attended by corpsmen, nurses, waves, and doctors. I'm getting better care than I got at Sampson for that matter, better than I got at Clark.

I don't feel like running races, but I don't feel ill. I get stabbed in the rump once every three hours with a hypo of penicillin by a corpsman who

---

5 *Not an entirely vain request. My grandfather probably had acquaintance with military higher-ups and political eminences of the time, and did occasionally intervene later with money and contacts. My uncle's frequent requests became more urgent as his service went on.*

6 *In a later letter, not included here, it emerges that my grandmother, in 1945, set a place for Jack at the Thanksgiving table, though he was far away in the South Pacific. He ridiculed the practice, if gently.*

must think he is an Olympian Greek with javelin. I'm fed pills and capsules and my nose is sprayed. I'm requested to drink water until I'm sure I've swallowed enough water to flood all of Russia. Everything is brought to me and I'm getting slightly tired of how intimate everyone is with my anatomy.

I've been tested for everything, almost, and by practically every means in the books.

From all of this you will gather that I don't think I'll be home this week-end and probably not the following one. Most of the patients stay here from two to three weeks.

I will undoubtedly be set back and be moved to another barracks. I won't know what class or barracks until I return to duty. Please write me here often, it's kind of lonely in this medicated mansion.

Don't worry about me. I'm really getting excellent care and I'll try to get well quickly.

Love,
Jack

*

23, Feb. '45

Dear Mother and Dad,

I received your letters today and there's one thing I want to state right away and that is that I'm not sick and I should be out of here next week. The only time I was at all sick, and then not really badly off, was the early part of this week. At present, I feel fine and itching to get out of here. We have ear-phones, through which we hear records and radio programs. We can snack in bed and I have plenty of reading matter, but I want to get out. The chow is terrible, the worse I've had at Bainbridge, but it's edible at times. I've gotten a lot of mail, but not because of being ill.

I went to sick bay Thursday and was transferred to the hospital Sunday evening. I still think that I don't and never had Scarlet Fever, but I can't tell them that.

I'm only getting stuck once every six hours now. I don't even notice it anymore. I'm getting used to it.

I think writing you postcards every day is a little silly,[7] as I'm perfectly all right.

---

[7] *Probably directed at my grandmother.*

As far as seeing me is concerned, I don't think it can be arranged and anyway I'll be home a week from tomorrow.

I think in general you've overestimated the seriousness of my ailment so please take restock and stop worrying.

Must close now. Please write often and remember I'm o.k.

Love,
Jack

*

Supply Officer
Naval Training Station
Bainbridge, Maryland
April 12, 1945

Dear Mother and Dad,

Well things don't look too good at this point since I've been set back. I've no alternative if I don't make fifteen by next Friday and to date I'm not up to par speed.[8] I am and will continue to work like a beaver (ran out of ink) for although I can't like the school and I don't want to be a radioman, neither do I want to wash out, even if it is only classed as an inaptitude. However, I want you to know that there is a very good possibility that I will wash out and I want you to be prepared for it. If it does happen I remain in schools unit for a few days on a working party, then I'll be transferred to Receiving and Sea unit to work there for a few days and then I'll be sent to O. G. U.[9] where I'll be reclassified. I may get another school or other duty, or I may be sent to general detail or, in other words, to sea as a swab jockey. Don't misunderstand me, I'm not anticipating anything but I want you to know what I'd do if I should be dropped. As I said, I don't like the idea of flunking and I do like the liberty so you can be sure that if I do flunk it won't be because I didn't try. Please let me know immediately when Dad gets home so that I can call him. I want to talk to him about this business.

I know this may sound pretty bad coming from someone my age but in this Navy you can't get anywhere unless you know someone who's in a fairly high place and who's willing to do something tangible for you. If you could only understand that without their help you get the short end of the stick

---

[8]*The test was in Morse Code.*

[9]*Out-going unit.*

every time. Don't any of your friends in Washington need a driver, guard, messenger, secretary or something? I mean it, I'd like a ship's company job somewhere in this area from which, in my spare time, I could work for a commission. It would seem to me that one of the people you know in D.C. could fix up something like that. I've talked to men here who are here because they had help. Don't misunderstand me, I'm not trying to avoid work, but I am trying to better myself and it can't be done, with my background and experience, without help from high places. I've proven to anyone that I can do a good job on anything I know about but I've got to have the chance. I realize that you don't like asking for favors and I have the same sense of pride but with many others doing it and getting places, and with things the way they are, I'm willing to cast pride to the winds. Please try and understand my point of view and let me know when I can call and talk it over with you.

Everything, except the code, is fine here. The weather is warm, though cloudy, and though the discipline is tightening up, one's off hours are still fairly pleasant.

Hope that everything is ok at home and that Dad and Peg had a good trip back. Must close now, write soon.

Love to all,
Jack.

*

United States Navy
July 3, 1945

Dear Parents,

Tomorrow is the fourth of July and for all the difference it will make to us it might as well be the tenth of August. I've got a ten to two watch coming up this evening so you can see how I'll spend the first two hours of independence day—didit, didit.[10]

We had a terrific storm yesterday afternoon and as a result today has been very pleasant, sunny, and warm but not in the least humid.

Friday we move to Sea Unit and will probably have liberty this weekend unless we get a really raw deal. Unless you hear otherwise from me I'll be

---

[10] *The "dots" of Morse Code. Dashes were "dah." By the month of July, Jack had been stateside for nine months, and the Pacific war was near its close.*

home. Do you think we could have an outdoor weenie roast if the weather permits? Even if the awning doesn't arrive we could move some of the furniture out on the porch and then put it back again. I'd like to spend a nice quiet weekend with you all and Sally.[11]

I don't particularly like the idea of not being able to come home and see you, even if it is brief, but I'm getting awfully damned fed up with the "U.S.S. Neversail" with all its pettyness and utter lack of anything military. You've got to go over to come back—let's shove off.

I don't know anything further about what or where I'll be assigned but as soon as I do I'll wire you, however, I'm sure that won't be until next week.

I want to get a little sleep before watch so I'll close for now, until Saturday, then—

Love to all,
Jack.

*

United States Navy
July 23, 1945

Dear Parents,

Yes I'm here[12] at last although I'd much rather be somewhere about three thousand miles east of here. The address on the envelope is not my permanent one but for the time being it will serve. The facilities here are a little on the crude side but still comfortable enough. There are many amusements available such as four movie theaters, two indoor swimming pools & one outdoor, several ships stores and soda fountains, a library[,] bowling alleys, tennis courts, gymnasiums, outdoors basket ball courts, and other things I haven't discovered as yet. If it weren't for the tremendous amount of men and conspicuously few women it would be somewhat like a summer resort. There is very little of the pettyness so evident at Sampson and Bainbridge and we're permitted to do pretty much as we please when we aren't going through processing. The weather here is very pleasant, it's hotter than blazes from about ten till five then it becomes gradually cooler until by the time one's ready to sleep two blankets are very comfortable.

They tell us that everyone here is going overseas and from what I've

---

[11] *The older woman my uncle was dating in Westchester.*

[12] *San Francisco, Calif.*

seen of the outgoing drafts they aren't kidding. I suppose I'll be leaving here in about two or three weeks of course I have no idea where or on what but I'll keep you well posted. Mention leave around here and the laughter can be heard in Frisco. So I'll see when I see a little—more likely a lot—of the shooting end of this war.

I hope you'll let me know about the people I can meet as soon as possible. We get only night liberties—the longest twenty-two hours—no weekends. We aren't permitted to travel further than fifty miles which includes the cities and towns around San Francisco. Further I hear that the civilians around here have seen just about enough sailors so knowing someone would make things a lot pleasanter.

The trip out was interesting if at times boring. The flood was at first exciting, later a pain in the neck. I spent an evening in the town of Dennis, Iowa, where I went to a dance and messed around in general. Going through Chicago and Denver I had [a] great desire to jump the train and visit the people I know but somehow I didn't get around to it. From Denver to here was especially interesting since I've never made it when able to appreciate it. Between Reno and Sacramento is some of the most beautiful country I've ever seen. Mountains, lakes, trout streams—everything for an ideal fishing trip.

Must lay over to the mess hall now for chow. I hope you'll write often even if I'm a little lax due to activity for the Navy.

Love to all,
Jack.

*

July 28, 1945

Dear Parents,

Well, I'm now in the chow hall again, we begin work this afternoon and I'm not too crazy about the idea. We work from two in the afternoon til about seven or eight in the morning from four-thirty til eight and ten til one then twenty-two hours of liberty. If we took all the liberty they gave us we'd be wrecks in a week. I went to San Francisco last night and arrived about ten minutes too late as far as getting in touch with any of the people whose names you gave me is concerned. Next time I'll call before I leave the base but yesterday I was a little over anxious to get away from the base—and unnecessarily so. I messed around the city til midnight and then returned to the base. It's really pretty lousy not knowing anyone.

At present I'm very broke with no pay in view—please wire some money immediately so that I can meet some of these people and spend some time with intelligent persons before the long months at sea or on the islands.

I'm glad the strike is over[13] and Dad can get some rest and a little recreation. I know I wouldn't like the job he's just successfully finished.

Tell Peg to keep working on the swimming and diving but not to forget her music while she's at it.

Must close now and start the drudgery. Write soon and often.

Love to all,
Jack.

*

United States Navy
August 19, 1945

Dear Parents,

Finally we've been graciously permitted to write.[14] I'd written several other letters but they contain information I'm forbidden to disclose at this time. I will send them when I can along with my new address as soon as I get one.

The news of the peace is marvelous but the stalling and general messing around that the Japs are engaged in now makes me feel slightly suspicious. When yours truly will get out is still a matter for discussion but it probably won't be very soon, there are still quite a few things to be attended to even if the war is over.

Life aboard ship is rather dull, as we are passengers and we have little to do and very little we can do. The living space is limited to say the least so as a result the small space we have is "Hotter 'n Hell" and I string my hammock on deck and snooze under the stars. The food is definitely the last

---

[13] *Labor problems at the Daily News. A considerable headache for my grandfather. Later, in the sixties, he developed serious heart trouble (though it was chronic long before) during a similar strike.*

[14] *Though Flynn often wrote a letter every day or two, there's a month-long gap preceding this note, while he is on the high seas. A significant month in global history, of course.*

word in dehydrated, powdered, and canned stuff, but really not too bad. We have movies every other night and although some are older than "Birth of a Nation" they are entertainment.

We haven't been told where we're going or what we'll do yet and I rather think the present situation has changed our original orders somewhat if not altogether. As soon as I know and am permitted I will tell you all the dope but as things stand now you know as much as I do.

I've received no mail since leaving Shoemaker and the prospects aren't very bright. We're only permitted to write on one sheet and use our Shoemaker address. Perhaps you'd better write to me at that address, they will forward it to me.

All in all, the present situation isn't too bad and at least they won't be shooting at us—I hope. I'd like to be back in the states, finishing my education and just being a civilian in general, but perhaps that day isn't too distant, at least I hope not. Give my best to all and write often.

Much love,
Jack.

*

Sept. 11, 1945

[A section is torn out of the letter, perhaps by censors aboard ship? Addressed to Peggy?]

... you may now refer ... as the beachcomber boy ... watched the communications tiers division of the Naval Operating Base Eniwetok atoll, Marshalls Island, Mic-Pacific Ocean, world. We were assigned to communications yesterday but we haven't moved to their barracks or started work due to the lack of space, however, we should move in the next couple of days.

Evening before last we worked as stevadores from six (PM) till three (AM) unloading L.C.T.'s[15] loaded with one-ton racks of landing strip matting. I almost became squashed Flynn when the idiot running the crane pulled the wrong lever. It was interesting, not too strenuous and something to do—an item we haven't indulged for almost two months.

There are many animals on the island which could not be listed under

---

[15] *Tank landing craft.*

the heading of natural fauna. Dogs, cats, and monkeys in abundance greet you at every turn. (missing section) . . . I suppose you're rather opposed to the idea of returning to the halls of learning but I personally would give everything to be able to do so.

Since the war is over I'm afraid I won't be able to bring you Jap souvenirs,[16] but I have picked up a few shells and bullets in the water off shore that were fired in the invasion of this island. They're all American for I'm afraid U.S. ships and men received all the Jap stuff, I'll try to get ahold of some for you thought it's pretty near impossible.

Please inform all of the people I know of my new address (dept. number follows in a couple of days) and ask them to write to this stranded sailor. Mail is absolutely the only connection with civilization we have. The radio and movies help but mail is a direct link.

You might also remind your mother to send any food stuff or (missing section). . . I hope you made a couple more successes in order to finish the season in a blaze of glory. I trust you will now turn you numerous talents toward the fields of music and the dance. Work at it and you won't be sorry, I guarantee you.

Well for lack of much to say I'll close now. In your letters be sure to raise questions. I'm sure I've failed to mention many things of interest and your questions will recall them to my mind. Write often and have a kind thought for your low-pointed brother.

Much love,
Jack

*

September 27, 1945

Dear Parents,

Well at present the mail seems to be getting somewhat regular, as of today I've received five letters. I wish there were some way for me to tell you how much mail means to us out here but it's just one of those things, if you're not here it seems a little ridiculous.

---

[16]*Traditional WWII enemy-baiting is leavened here slightly by the fact that my uncle was born in Tokyo, during the twenties when my grandfather was located there as a stringer, among other things. Family lore has it that the telegram announcing Jack's birth arrived in New York the day before he was born, because of the date line.*

As a matter of fact, unless this island is abandoned I see no immediate change of duty for your young son. I've tried several times to get into the occupational forces but to no avail. I'm here for permanent duty until released by the powers that are.

I'd like very much to be able to help you (Dad) in whatever the problems may be but I don't see how I possibly could, I don't seem to have the right attitude for it. My big desire is to write[17] and you can't do much of that russing about an office, believe me I know. However, if when I get back and finish college you think I can be of any assistance I'll be very flattered to try.

My dear woman, if you've ever seen on of these "nice" huts and the cots we sleep on you wouldn't refer to them in the manner you have. It is, without a doubt the closest thing to living in a rabbit hutch I'll ever come to know—I hope. With all the many and varied domestic problems I'll still take little old Pelham.

Give Peg my love and best wishes as a great model, I too wish I could be present at the showing of so lovely a little lady.

There isn't much to relate about happenings here, I arise in the morning, wash in a helmet with water collected from roof when it rains—which is rather indefinite at best—eat breakfast with mess gear which was issued to us when we first arrived, tidy up the hut and off to the office. After four hours of typing up discharge cards I am the lucky recipient of an hour off for lunch, then back to the sweat shop for another four hours. Upon my return to the hut after consuming a couple of beers or cokes as the mood strikes me (now I can be particular) I again use the helmet in an attempt to shower, it's a failure as a shower but somehow or another I get clean. Again I eat, rotten habit I got into when I was very young, then I either dope off in the sack, attend a movie which I may or may not have seen, depending on whether or not it's old or ancient, read, or write letters. As you can see it's a thrilling existence and has much room for improvement. However, occasionally, one runs into something rather interesting, for instance yesterday I had the honor of meeting the son of the chief of the Eniwetok tribe of natives. They have all been moved to an island out of reach of amorous sailors but occasionally the chief visits the great white father (the captain) and we see the people who actually want to live here, why I haven't the slightest idea but who am I to argue with people whose ancestors sailed over thousands of miles of ocean in outrigger canoes to get here. I realize my descriptions are brief and vague at best so please ask questions and I'll do my best to answer them.

---

[17] One of many points of contact for me with the author of letters. Despite ambitions in this direction and demonstrable talent, this correspondence is a large part of Jack Flynn's surviving written work.

UNITED STATES NAVY

August 19, 1945

Dear Parents,

Finally we've been graciously permitted to write. I've written several other letters but they contain information I'm forbidden to disclose at this time. I will send them when I can along with my new address as soon I got one.

The news of the peace is marvelous but the stalling and general messing around that the Japs are engaged in now makes me feel slightly suspicious. When yours truly will get out is still a matter for discussion but it probably won't be very soon, there are still quite a few things to be attended to even if the war is over.

Life aboard ship is rather dull, as we are passengers we have very little to do and very little we can do. The living space is limited to say the least so as a result the small space we have is "Hotter 'n Hell" and I string my hammock on deck and snooze under the stars. The food is definitely the last word in dehydrated, powdered, and canned stuff but really not too bad. We have movies every other night, and although some are older than "a birth of a nation" they are entertainment.

We haven't been told where we're going or what we'll do yet and I rather think the present situation has changed our original orders somewhat if not altogether. As soon as I know and am permitted I tell you all the dope but as things stand now you know as much as I do.

We've received no mail since leaving Shoemaker and the prospects aren't very bright. We're only permitted to write on one sheet and use our Shoemaker address. Perhaps you'd better write to me at that address, they will forward it to me.

All in all the present situation isn't too bad and at least they won't be shooting at us — I hope. I'd like to be back in the states, finishing my education and just being a civilian in general but perhaps that day isn't too distant, at least I hope not. Give my best to all and write often.

Much love, Jack

Don't forget the idea of buying a piece of the great north woods and building a camp there, I find that idea comes more and more often into my head and I like it a lot. Nothing could be better in my opinion.

Well I'll sign off now with the request that you write often and remember that it won't be long now.

Much love to all,
Jack

*

October 21 [1945]

Dear Parents,

At this time I suppose I could tell innumerable lies but the truth is I've been demoted—reason—arguing with the boss (Lt.). I honestly don't fully understand it, he said that if I'd been insolent he['d] had thrown me in the brig so I wasn't that. He further said if I proved by work and silence that I was a good boy he'd give my first class back to me. I don't fully understand what I did or failed to do that netted me this reward. For myself I don't give a tinker's dawn, but I hate to disappoint and let you down. I'll make good for you yet but I'm going to have to throw my own principles, ideals, and ideas out to do it. There are certain things, such as boot-licking, I don't subscribe to. Oh yes, I may be transferred from here but it's not very indefinite. I may or may not and as to the when & where, of course I haven't the slightest idea.

If you were to ask me now I'd say I've not slacked work—more than usual—or said or done anything wrong, but then I may not see what was wrong. At any rate I will work doubly hard and say nothing and attempt to regain my rate and good standing. Remember I have no bad marks against my record, all this is unofficial and just between the Lt. and myself.

I'll do my best to learn and appreciate this experience, as you call it. I find many things of interest out here and I'm not wholly bored and disgusted. I've learned more about real values, and the thing—people—since I've been in the Navy than I would have in my whole life otherwise. I'm grateful for that much of this mess.

I suppose it's about time I told you a lot of things that will help you understand your errant son a little better. First, I've known, for my age, a lot of girls and have had, as you charmingly put it, experiences and still maintain that it's not much and yours truly can do without it. I've never clicked or gotten along with any girl more than superficially, it seems my eccentricities get a trifle dull after a bit. My personal opinion is that no girl will ever wish to inflict my personal kind of torture on herself for very long. However, be that as it may I've been unofficially engaged since June,[18] yes, yes I know. Don't get any misimpressions, the idiot understands fully that I've got at least a four-year education to acquire and God knows how many years wait until I'm set. I said idiot advisedly. Any girl who would attach herself to someone like me must be an idiot. I think that when she knows a lad who is other than a romantic thirty-six-hour-pass sailor she'll change her mind but I hope she doesn't. I love her. Have no fears about any rash moves, one—she has a lot more practically than I have, two—I won't support anyone in any other manner the one to which I'm accustomed. That subject now opened I move on.

I think that I'll be out by next year at this time. I'm hoping to get out in time to start college—keep your fingers crossed.

I work under a staff filled with gold braid, I'm directly responsible to a Lt. whom I've already mentioned. There are about fifteen rated yeomen also working there. The brunt of all administrative work falls on their shoulders. The entire atoll has eight thousand some odd men. Peacetime strength will be something like four-hundred men and twenty-seven officers. I'm not sure how long the Navy intends to keep this bit of sand, however, I do know they're going to keep it for a while. I could tell you a million little stories of Navy inefficiency and wastefulness, but I only know the enlisted man's side of it all and I don't think they're very important.

There's not much else to report. Life continues apace with Flynn in the doghouse attempting to extricate himself. Write often and think of me kindly. I'm really a good lad at heart.

Much love to all,
Jack

*

November 1, 1945

Dear Parents,

Received the two postcards from Dad, a letter and some humorous clippings from Mother. Hope that I'll be able to be of some assistance to the

---

[18]Unclear if this refers to Sally, his girlfriend above, or to another woman friend encountered during military service.

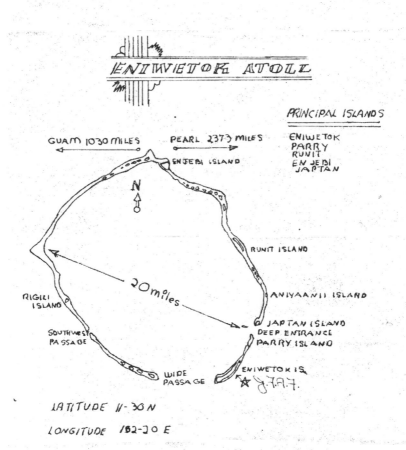

ENIWETOK ATOLL

PRINCIPAL ISLANDS

ENIWETOK
PARRY
RUNIT
ENJEBI
JAPTAN

GUAM 1030 MILES — PEARL 2373 MILES →

ENJEBI ISLAND

N

20 miles

RUNIT ISLAND

ANIYAANII ISLAND

RIGILI ISLAND

JAPTAN ISLAND
DEEP ENTRANCE
PARRY ISLAND

SOUTHWEST PASSAGE

WIDE PASSAGE

ENIWETOK IS.
☆ J.F.F.

LATITUDE 11-30 N

LONGITUDE 162-30 E

Map of Eniwetok Atoll, hand-drawn, by Flynn himself

newspaper world in regard to its labor troubles although at present I know little or nothing about the situation or should I say situations.

Speaking of glasses I'm to get some soon—free from the Navy—or did I tell you? They told me that I was farsighted, however I've still got twenty-twenty vision. I don't understand how they arrive at that solution, but "there are more things on heaven and earth . . ." etc.

Tomorrow or the next day we're moving anchorage which means taking on supplies and going somewhere. To the states seems to be the current thought. If we don't stop at Pearl Harbor I may be in the states soon. However, I personally don't think I could be that lucky. I foresee another change of duty soon. Of course I'm hoping and keeping my fingers crossed but it just doesn't seem possible—it's too good.

I can't repeat too often how much I like this ship and the men concerned—in all a very good deal. I'm improving with the code, etc. Soon, I should be standing watches alone.

I hope you'll forgive the fitful writing but I don't have a great deal of free time and then sometimes I just don't feel like writing[.] [I]t all seems so damn silly just trivial chatter while the world staggers along to the next mass slaughter. Push a button and puff no London.[19] Just a question of time and who pushes the first button. Oh, what a laugh—freedom, does it really exist anywhere? The years of reconstruction and proud talk of disarmament and eternal peace—does anyone think it will happen—can anyone be that innocently naïve? Forgive me, but I wonder if there's any point in the whole business of life and living. There doesn't seem to be. Well, I suppose you think I'm in a mood, perhaps I am but still I wonder, do you?

Write soon and often and keep the home fires burning, after this climate I'll need warmth.

Love to all,
Jack

*

November 21, 1945

Dear Parents,

Tomorrow we will eat Thanksgiving dinner on the high seas on route to Majuro atoll. We are carrying eighty-three passengers and a load of lum-

---

[19] *When I first read these letters, I was surprised at the absence of the Japanese atomic blasts from the month of August as rendered here. This paragraph includes the only mention. Perhaps the material was censored by the authorities, or perhaps by Jack himself.*

ber. We arrive at six (approximately) Friday morning and by noon we are supposed to unload the wood, disembark the passengers, embark three hundred more and be underway for the return trip here. Quite a job, I'd say but that's the story[.] [U]pon returning here with the passengers we disembark them and head for Ponape where we pick up natives, British subjects, and take them to the crown colony at Ocean island. Ocean is south of the equator so it would seem your son will receive his initiation into the Grand Order of Shellbacks. After Ocean we return for more natives at Ponape to be taken back to Ocean. We then return to Ponape to pickup Jap prisoners for delivery to Yokahama. We deliver British subjects and Jap subjects while there isn't enough transportation to get Americans home—some deal! Personally it sounds interesting, I think I'll like it, but it just isn't playing smart.

So then it's Kwajalein to Majuro and back (231 miles each way), Kwajalein to Ponape (576 m.), Ponape to Ocean (827 m.) and back, Ponape to Ocean and back, and then Ponape to Yokahama (2,759 m.). In all, seven thousand ninety-seven miles of Pacific Ocean to travel and then who knows how much more. I'm anxious to see Japan and I hope the ship holds together til we get there. Please give me the names of anyone you know there so that if we make a few liberties I can meet them.

Also I'd advise a loud squawk in the press about using an American ship manned by nineteen-month veterans to take Japs home while our men stay out here.

Write often.

Love to all,
Jack

*

November 28, 1945

Dear Mother and Dad,

Received a three page letter from Dad this noon. Sorry here that things seem to be following the expected course; but at least this we've known all along that our being out here wouldn't do a hell of a lot of good.

I don't quite understand why every time I mention a girl it follows that I must receive a brief lecture[20] on returning to school and getting a good start before thinking of any entanglement. In the first place I intend to go

---

[20]*Not an unusual situation, apparently: my grandfather lecturing my uncle.*

back to school but not because you think it's best but because I think it's best. Secondly, I'm no more fooled by the fallacy of "two can live as cheaply as one" than you are and I'm not at all anxious to be responsible for someone else's life. Paralleling that I'm not too sure that I'll find anyone willing to live my way with me. I think I may have but I also think she's too young to know what she wants—that will work out in time. Thirdly, even if I was idiot enough to want to marry right away, I would. I'm living my life, you're not, and although I value and need your advice please remember that that's all it is. I like you a lot and it's not a paternal-son sort of thing. I admire your mind and ability, if I could be as much of a person I'd be very happy. You and I have had and could have a very happy time but let's not botch it up with a lot of ideas that are yours, not mine, on my life. I'll always want your opinion and views and will probably need your help for a while but please remember that I'm F. A. Flynn, not a second edition of F. M. & not quite the infant with moody ideas that you seem to think; my experience is small but I daresay a bit larger than yours at my age—by the way, the age of a college sophomore. This is my second year in the Navy. I have ideas and convictions which I believe just as strongly as you believe yours, I still seek new solutions and need a great deal of education but I'm an entity.

I agree that there isn't much I can do about conditions but I'm going to try and find out what the majority want and then I'll butt my head against a wall trying to help them get it—typical youthful fervor but I'm an idealist and can't help it.

I don't think, however, that thinking that not many people know what's going on is just a phase, they don't, not even when their lives are pawns for military chessmasters. You're lucky you've an educated and brilliant mind but talk to a few who haven't. I know, I live with them.

Write often and get us home, we're not doing a damn thing here.

Love to all,
Jack

*

San Francisco
Jan 3, 1946

Dear Parents,

Well I expect that by the time this arrives you'll have heard from me I have liberty tomorrow and I plan to call you. I received your Christmas wire this morning when I went on watch (0345—3:45 AM) and numerous letters but there are gaps, that is, I've some rather recent ones which refer to some I haven't got at all. I suppose they'll catch up with me sometime.

What the future holds in store for your roving son I can only guess. Leave? Back at sea? East Coast? Shore duty? Who knows. I'm sure I don't! I'm hoping for a leave but I don't see much light in that direction. I'd like to get duty somewhere near home or at least in the U.S. but unless you can do something about that I don't see much hope there either. In other words, at this writing there are many things I'd like to know which I don't, and many things I'd like to do which seem out of reach.

I have no idea how long we'll be here or what we'll do. We may decommission the ship, if so it may be here or on the East Coast. The ship may be overhauled and sent to sea with your low-pointed son. She may be used as a coast-wise cargo ship—who knows? I hope by tomorrow to have a little more information but you can rest assured that what I know you'll know very soon thereafter.

Most of the men on board are or will be eligible for discharge. At any rate they deserve a leave and should get it. I think I will before going back overseas if I do, but whether from this ship or some other command I don't know. Don't count on it, I'm not.

We arrived at Pearl on the morning of the twenty-first of December and left in the evening of the twenty-fourth. I had two liberties there and didn't have what you'd call a thrilling time. Aside from these two slight contacts you suggested I was strictly on my own. I bought a few things, ate a couple of steaks, drank milk (and other things) and looked the place over in general. Our liberties were only eleven hours long, noon till eleven so I didn't see a great deal. I went to the famous Wakaki Beach and thought it much overrated—I'll take Nassau. It might be better though with half a million fewer sailors. In brief, I'd say Honolulu is much better than a coral atoll but is not quite the states but could be seen better in civilian clothes.

As I think I've said, at present I don't know the score—or even who's playing—and lack of sleep and a lot of unnecessary work make me feel a little annoyed. However, as soon as I know anything I'll let you know.

Please don't send any packages until I get an idea of what's going on or unless I ask for something.

Keep writing and I'll do the same.

Love to all,
Jack

*

January 5, 1946

Dear Mother and Dad,

Talking to you last night was really a shot in the arm, after a while this life of routine and subjugation puts one in a rather downcast frame of mind. Hearing your voices again lifted me to tops of the now barren trees. I can't thank you enough for letting me call[,] for setting things up for me here, and for just being you.

I saw quite a few men wearing honorable discharge buttons (an honor I'd like to be permitted) and a surprising number of the wearers were bums, asking for handouts and telling sad tales. Doesn't speak well of the glorious G.I. Bill of Rights and other veterans advantages we've heard so much about. However, the city still seemed strained and overcrowded as it was during the war. Perhaps I didn't interpret correctly or see enough but it still had the air of militarism and war so far as I could see. The hills and docks around the harbor have large signs loudly proclaiming welcome and well done but no one seemed overjoyed to see us.

Tell Peg that I'm sending some more junk home including my battle helmet which is now useless and never served me for anything but a wash basin. The lad that had it before me may have stopped bullets with it but the only thing it saved me from was comfort.

Will write again and inform you as to the results of my liberty and late bulletins concerning our disposition.

Love to all,
Jack

*

January 18, 1946

Dear Dad,

Undoubtedly you, by this time, think me mad but I assure you that I'm far from that stage. However, I am in a bit of a dilemma, this damn town is too high-priced. Nonetheless, if you want me to rot aboard ship as I did for six months out in the Pacific or to follow the seedy, sordid, highly unsatisfactory life of a sailor on liberty in San F[r]an then you can pay no attention to my request for funds. I sent you my estimate on what liberty costs and I'm sure you'll find that it's conservative if you check with your friends here.

You'll say perhaps that I had a pretty good time in N.Y.C. without going through so much green stuff but I'm sure prices here are higher and then too I had a home to return to and you oiled the way for me in many cases.

One reason that I'm in need of money right now is that yesterday I was sent to San Fran as an official courier to obtain dispatches and messages. While I was gone the ship was paid so I missed out on that. You can confirm this by wiring Lt. G. B. Wolf, our captain.

If you don't think you should send me money I wish you'd do me the favor of contacting my bank and drawing that money for me or cashing some of the bonds I've had sent home. In any case, some day I'll be in a position to repay you and I assure you that I will.

When and if I get back to the east coast I'll withdraw into an inexpensive shell but in this town that's impossible, impossible that is if you want to live like a human being.

I talked to the skipper yesterday and he said that no one of the gold ashore knows anything about our future movements. At present we're waiting for dispatch orders from chief of naval operations. Anyway it would seem that we're here for a while.

I've been having a pretty good time on liberties with Mildred who is really a sweet girl, I'm sure you'd both like her very much, even if she does work for Hearst.

Must buzz off now, please try to consider from my standpoint and don't become too angry.

Love to all,
Jack

*

United States Navy
February 2, 1946

Dear Parents,

Received Dad's letter of the twenty-ninth and am very grateful for the money order, thanks a million. I know that I'm a hell of a drain on the exchecker but I'm trying to cut the expenses to the bone. I'm not expecting anything in the way of entertainment of excitement, I'm just trying to find things to do on liberty that are somewhat like the things I did at home. Frankly the simple things that I did when I was at home are the things I wish I could find here. I'm not worried about what I do here, I'm just looking for things familiar and inexpensive. I'd try the fishing deal if we ever got liberty early enough in the day to do so, but with the exception of one day a week, all our liberties are overnight.

I talked to the skipper this afternoon and sounded him on the possibilities of leave etc. and it would seem that there's still hope and he further said we'll be on this coast for some time. Since he lives in Los Angeles he's trying to get the ship moved down there but how successful he will be I don't know. Of course, after hearing you say that you had some really good connections down there I'm in favor one hundred percent.

If you're not too opposed to the idea and it can be worked out, I'd like to ask for that beautiful Ford. With gas rationing over and the Caddy in excellent condition you wouldn't need the Ford. Further there must be someone of our acquaintance that would like to drive to their destination here, that is surely someone of the News men or some friend is headed out this way and driving out seems to me a swell way to get cross country. I'm sure that the cost of gas, oil, and general upkeep won't be more than transportation prices out here. The skipper has also [said] that if we do go south his sister would be glad to drive it down there and in the event we go somewhere really distant I'm sure Mr. Fitzpatrick or one of the other gentleman wouldn't mind taking care of it for a while. Also the Capt. said we could even take it aboard ship if I so desired. If you want confirmation write him and inquire. I don't doubt that you think I'm completely nuts but I think it's a darn good idea. If someone already coming out here drove it out—no cost, I can keep it in Navy garages—not cost (and with friends in San Fran.—no mon.) upon the event of a leave I'll drive it back—no cost or if not I'll be discharged someday and then I'll bring it back, costs here would exclude all existing transportation expenses and probably quite a few others—I'm happy just driving around. I may be wrong but I don't think it will inconvenience you any, in any event let me know what you think of the idea and if possible take action on it as quickly as expedient.[21]

Will close now with wishes for recovery of Dad and Peg from their colds and prayers that Mama won't catch anything. Write soon—

Love to all,
[unsigned]

---

21 *The car comes up often in later missives.*

USS LST 689
Fleet Post Office
San Francisco, California.
[undated, probably late March or April 1946]

Dear Parents,

Sorry I was unable to get in touch with you last night but I hadn't anything really important to say anyway. I just wanted to tell you that I am changing jobs aboard ship although that will not have any effect on my rating if I ever get one. The lad that was acting as our storekeeper left yesterday for discharge and since the ship is in for decommissioning we can't get any replacements so the Capt. elected me to fill in for the nonce. It will mean a change of hours which I am going to like—no more watches in the middle of the night—a full night in the sack—I can't remember the last time I had one. The work of being a storekeeper itself isn't hard and it will give me opportunity to get off the ship more often and see some of the Naval shore bases in the Bay Area. Further I'll perhaps learn something about things which I know nothing of at present. I'll tell you more of the setup when I've been at it for a short time. All I can say now is that I like the idea and I think it will be a good change.

What about the car, have you decided just to ignore the idea or have you been so busy that you couldn't write? On the other hand the mail has been rather fouled up recently[;] perhaps your letters haven't caught up as yet. However, I wish you'd let me know as soon as possible about your ideas on the subject and I hope you are in favor of the idea because I know it would be a good thing.

Liberty continues to be very nice and I'm having a swell time. Total expenditures last night were one dollar and fifty cents—an amazing event. I had dinner at Mildred's home with her family, a charming group of people and then we just messed around until about mid-night when I returned to the hotel for a little of that wonderful stuff called sleep.

Well I must close now for I must make a trip to obtain our pay accounts and find out where and when the ship will get paid. Write soon and often—

Love to all,
[unsigned]

*

USS LST 689
9, April 1946[22]

Dear Mother,

Departed Astoria at eight this morning and are now underway up the Columbia River for Portland. We should arrive there late this afternoon or evening, as I told you in my wire last night, our address has been changed and is now, U.S.S. LST 689 c/o Main Post Office, Portland, Oregon. It's a miserable day, rain and fog with a very heavy overcast, so the trip isn't as interesting as it might have been. The country up here reminds me a great deal of Canada, wooded hills and a clear invigorating air about it.

My reason for asking you to disregard the mention of transfer in my last letter was that whether or not I'm on sea duty will make only fifteen days difference in my discharge and the leave is doubtful in any event. On last check, I'm eligible for discharge on the fifteenth of June if I remain on sea duty and the first of July if I do not. So if a transfer is possible to somewhere near—with liberty distance—of home I'd like it. Hope I haven't caused any inconvenience with a quick and unreasoning letter but at the time I wrote it I was doing so under a misapprehension.

I wrote the U. of M. today asking if I could still get in there this fall. According to what I've heard, state institutions are not accepting non-resident students. However, I mentioned their letter to me in '44 in which they said I would acceptable when I could enter and also that you and Dad had both attended and lived in Missouri. Do we own any property in Missouri, the skipper said it might help if we paid taxes to the state, what do you think?

I'm still working as a poor substitute for a yeoman and disliking it more as each day passes, it's vital and necessary to the ship and crew so I'll stick with it and do the best I can until I leave the ship or until the get a competent man. At present I'm on watch guarding a voice frequency over which nothing is coming in, very dull! However, a relief from that rotten office.

The weather is clearing up so perhaps I'll be able to get a few pictures of this famous and picturesque river. However, from all indications and reports this is the season for rain in "these hear parts" and I'll vote for that from what I've seen thus far.

---

[22] *The last of the extant letters, for the reason that Francis Arthur Flynn, able-bodied seaman, was soon discharged from the Navy.*

Will close now as garbled sounds are reaching my ears, write soon and often and get Peg to sit down for a few minutes and scratch me out a note.

Love to all[23]

---

[23] *Why be interested in a footnote to WWII? In the life of a distant relative in a period comprised mainly of his own tedium and homesickness? Maybe because of sentences like the above, sentences in which the thrust of life as lived is evident. Not the lives of generals, not eyewitness accounts of Pacific sieges, but the lives of characters constructed in minutiae, rain water in a combat helmet, a body floating in the San Francisco Bay, an unused place-setting at the Thanksgiving dinner table, scarlet fever, neglected atolls, the wilted passions that might attend such things. This is enough, for me, because in it I can feel for myself the inadequacy of imagination when compared to how character reveals itself in truth. Have I ever fictionally imagined a man who is revealed as fully as my uncle is revealed in these pages? I don't think so. And I feel the failure acutely.*

This would be reason enough to excerpt these letters and to invite others to have a look, but it's not the only reason. I'm also fascinated by these letters because I know what happens after their close. Which is that my uncle attempts to go to college for a while, and then gives up. First because he can't stand St. Louis and, later, because the Jesuits at Fordham irritate him. Instead, after hanging around the family homestead until ejected by my grandfather, he gets into the television business, at the ground level, in L.A. and later Chicago and New York City. Despite wearing a lot of hats in the early years of t.v., reporter, announcer, etc., he eventually settles into a life as a television advertising salesman, a job at which he is very effective. He is married and he and his wife raise a daughter and son, my cousins. He divorces his first wife, after some heartache, and marries again. There is rumor of a drinking problem, or at least some very heavy drinking, and it wouldn't be hard to imagine, since my grandmother, by the late 1950s, has already succumbed to a cycle of drying-out joints and hospitalizations. But this isn't the really sad part, the sad part is that my uncle stopped drinking and was apparently doing quite well for himself when he took a certain 727 to Cincinnati, OH, in 1965, along with a regional ad salesman from WPIX, whereupon the jet went down, in fog, and struck a hillside, losing all the lives aboard.

Lots to despise in a story like this. Cincinnati, for example. Cincinnati is innocent, but I hate it anyhow, and when I have been there in my adult life, I have felt a coiled disgust in me always. When Cincinnati proved its cultural mettle during the Maplethorpe controversy, or during the reign of Marge Schott (owner of the Cincinnati Reds) something in me leapt up. A hideous place, which deserved its fate, as in the spring 2001 riots. And beyond Cincinnati, there is the Navy to despise, because they borrowed and never returned two years of my uncle's life in order to prosecute a war, in order to slaughter civilians, and he might otherwise have spent these two years doing all the things that young people justifiably do when they are eighteen and nineteen, going to the theater and to baseball games, driving around with myriad girlfriends. Then there's the airlines to hate, and the television business, for necessitating his travel that day, and so forth. Yet no amount of rage seems to expend this noxious fuel of disappointment.

I remember him fitfully, from Christmas Day celebrations in Darien, where we were living (he sat crossly on sofa), from a weekend at his beach house in West Hampton, on Long Island. He had a house on stilts. There were many dunes. I am not sure if these are real memories or imaginings suggested by photos and stories.

For years after his death, my mother saw him on the street, a certain cast of the head, a certain gait. Upon inspection, it was not my uncle. But the obliteration that goes with jet crashes, as with othr sudden deaths, entails that the lost beloved will inhabit passers-by and old haunts for many years after. All the promise of a young writer who made it out of the war unscathed, who wasn't dumped into the Pacific to be fed upon by sharks, nor maimed at Guadalcanal, nor witness to the aftermath of the bombing of Tokyo, nor part of the occupying force in Japan, all this promise is vanished on the plane in Cincinnati. When my uncle was still younger than I am now.

Seeing him in these letters, imagining him at their close, discharged, driving his Ford around the West Coast with some money in his pocket, how hard it is not to think that much sadnesses would lie ahead. In these pages, the war, for all its enormity, is a false-ending, a tease. What is the garbled sound reaching his ears then? Of which he speaks? Just more dots and dashes from the radio? Or something else? An emblem for how we march onward, through trenches, dimly aware of our vulnerability. ✧

What is the Color of Hope in Haiti?

Jason Wilson

"This was not the tourist season, and in any case the island to which we
were bound was no longer an attraction for tourists."
—*Graham Greene, The Comedians*

Brown is the color of Haiti's mountainous spine. Not a lovely sepia or a
deep mahogany, mind you, but a flat, sickly, heartbreaking brown. Mile
after mile of slopes and valleys bake in the hot sun with no trees, no crops,
no sign of life whatsoever. In less than a century, Haiti's interior has gone
from a lush agricultural center—once prized by French colonialists for its
coffee and sugar—to a desert, stripped bare of any timber that might possibly be burned for fuel or used to build shelter. You can see the skeletal
remains of the forests carried down the roads as dry dead twigs on the
heads and backs of broken men and women. Haitians chop down nearly 30
million of their trees each year.

I could tell you that my visit to Haiti comes back to me in the vibrant
reds and blues and yellows of the crazy *tap-taps,* carrying sardined passengers over streams of raw sewage in the overcrowded streets of Port-au-
Prince, windshields emblazoned with sayings like "Merci, Jesus" or
"Lamentations 3:26" or "Sylvester Stallone." I could say that it comes back
to me in the gold and purple papier-mâché masks of Carnival in Jacmel or
the sunny, hand-painted placemats found on every table in every restau-
rant. Or that it comes back in the blood red of the blackjack tables at the El
Rancho in Petionville, rumored to be a hangout of drug kingpins, where
my friend Míchel won $800 our first night, where a faded pink $5 chip fell
out of my pocket, and where a teenage prostitute dove to the carpet in front
of me to grab it. I could tell you that Haiti comes back to me in the simple
word "blanc" that little children would scream at the sight of our white
faces each time we passed through villages in our truck.

All those colors are true. But to truly understand the plight of Haiti—
the poorest country in the Western Hemisphere, a place where 75 percent
of the people live in absolute poverty—you need to understand brown.

A dusty brown that covers your shoes and clothes and bags from the
moment you are greeted first by the creaky brass band on the tarmac at the
Port-au-Prince airport, then by the sign at customs that reads, "We Are
Sorry To Welcome You In This Condition." It's the same brown as the hide
of the mangy, rabid dog we saw fighting with an enormous pig over the

right to eat a pile of garbage—this in the middle of an alley that Saíntil, our driver, used as a short cut to navigate Port-au-Prince traffic. It's the brown of dirty rivers where women and children bathe and do laundry and relieve themselves, only a few hundred yards upstream from the food stalls of an open-air market.

Brown is the color of Haiti's dry, suffering present.

"Yet, even amid all the brown, a glimmer of hope for the country's future may be seen in a new color—blue. More specifically, *bleu*, as in Haitian Bleu, a new variety of gourmet coffee bean now being grown by Haiti's highland coffee farmers." I wrote that, three years ago. And I will freely admit that I embellished, if not outright lied, in that passage.

My sole excuse: I wanted desperately to write a positive story about Haiti. I had come to report on the Haitian Bleu coffee-growing project, which quite possibly might have been the only positive story about Haiti that would appear all year in the American press.

The Haitian Bleu project sounded great in theory. Funded by the U.S. Agency for International Development, and administered locally by the Inter-American Institute for Cooperation in Agriculture, the project educates coffee farmers in Haiti's remote highlands in the development, planting, pruning, and harvesting of gourmet coffee. The mission is twofold: IICA hopes to create a profitable cash crop for people who desperately need the money, and, because high-quality shade coffee needs larger trees to thrive, a powerful incentive to save what's left of Haiti's remaining forests is also created. IICA trains these farmers, who previously used crude slash-and-burn techniques, how to grow high-quality coffee the correct way. Many see this education as the key to saving Haiti's dwindling environment. One of the great things about Haitian Bleu is you have to plant trees, said the do-gooders at IICA.

Haiti once produced a well-regarded coffee, and the crop accounted for nearly 80 percent of the nation's GNP, but the industry fell on hard times earlier in this century. Exporters consumed profits and exploited farmers, paying them lower prices without reinvesting money into the product. This vicious cycle resulted in a poor-quality coffee product, which had such a bad reputation that it could only be consumed locally, or else it was shipped across the border and sold as Dominican Republic coffee.

"Long ago, the export houses formed a cartel. They buy together and control the price," said Stéphan Jean-Pierre, Haitian Bleu's business manager. The Haitian Bleu project attempts to circumvent the traditional chain of middlemen by allowing cooperatives of coffee growers—organized under the name Caféiéres Natíves—to deal directly with roasters in the

United States. There is, of course, always fear of political retribution from the traditional export cartel, but in a half dozen years, the Caféiéres Natíves grew to include more than 19,000 farmers. These farmers, who once made only 80 cents per pound for their coffee, now made an average of $2 per pound. Perhaps that doesn't sound like much improvement, but remember, Haiti's annual per capita income is $370. Money wired from the United States, nearly $3 million a day, was considered the largest source of hard currency in Haiti. A more candid American consultant told me that Haitian Bleu had been created on shaky ground from the beginning. For one thing, she said, it's very hard to find reliable figures for how much coffee is actually grown and sold. "It's impossible to measure. It's on baskets; it's on donkeys," she said. "A peasant farmer in Haiti doesn't keep books." So even if Haitian Bleu represented hope for the future, the future at that time was still a long way off.

What about now? Anyone who reads the newspaper knows that Haiti is aflame in chaos right now. Jean-Bertrand Aristide has returned to power, and the international community has frozen millions of dollars in aid due to charges of a tainted election. Aristide supporters shut down Port-au-Prince by burning tires and throwing stones at cars. The opposition has named a "provisional president." Random violence between Aristide's supporters and those who accuse him of returning Haiti to a dictatorship has spread to the countryside. Coffee and people cutting down trees are perhaps the least of anyone's concern.

Looking back on my visit now, I realize how misguided my plans turned out to be. How silly it was to think I'd jet in for five days, collect some information, drive through the coffee fields, shoot some photos, and scoot out with an uplifting narrative. Now it is more than three years later, and if you talk to coffee buyers and tasters, they will tell you that Haitian Bleu is really, at best, a mediocre coffee. Some say it leaves much too bitter of an aftertaste.

I came to Haiti with Kevin and Míchel, two *blancs* twice my age who tagged along for an adventure—our odd group resembling the doomed trio in Graham Greene's novel about Haiti, *The Comedians*. IICA simply lent us a truck and a 49-year-old driver named Saíntil and sent us driving south to Jacmel, which would be our home base for the next few days.

As we puttered along in the bumper-to-bumper Port-au-Prince traffic, Saíntil surprised us by saying he often longs for a day when Papa Doc Duvalier, with his voodoo mysticism and his dreaded secret police, the murderous Tontons Macoutes, would be returned to power and end the utter chaos and lawlessness that exists today. Saíntil said this even though he was certainly old enough to remember first-hand the terrible violence of the Duvalier regime. "Many people believe that Papa Doc is still alive," he said. "No one actually saw him buried in his coffin. People say they've seen him, late at night, walking the streets of Port-au-Prince."

We needed to exchange dollars for *gourdes,* so Saíntil cut out of traffic and sped through several backstreets. He eventually pulled the truck through a metal gate at a grey, nondescript warehouse, past several armed guards, and parked. The four of us entered a dimly lit backroom where a woman and two men were counting piles upon piles of money—gourdes, dollars, and any number of other currencies. Without so much as a word, the woman quickly took our twenties and fifties, counted out gourdes, and handed them to us. The two men never looked up as they continued to wrap piles of bills in rubber bands. Three minutes later, we were escorted back outside and straight to the truck by one of the armed guards. "Let's just not ask questions," Kevin said to me. "Just don't ask any questions."

The trip to Jacmel, which was only about sixty kilometers away, took over five hours. First, Kevin and Míchel requested a beer stop, and Saíntil pulled over at the Snack Bar De L'Immaculee Conception. After we finished one, everyone decided to take another one for the road. Saíntil threw his empty beer bottle out the driver's side window. "I guess littering isn't against the law here?" Kevin asked with a chuckle.

"Law?" said Saíntil. "There are no laws in Haiti."

I don't know what was more painful as we traversed our way to Jacmel—the bone-jarring depressions and potholes along the road or looking at the dry, parched mountains we passed.

It was early evening by the time we arrived in Jacmel. Guides, truck-watchers, and people selling fruit and wooden sculptures swarmed outside our hotel. We hired a boy no older than twelve to take us around town and, within the hour he dragged out his slightly older "sister" and offered her up to the highest bidder for the evening.

Guides would continue to hound us throughout the next several days. At one point, when we needed to find a telephone, we had to hire three guides, one for each of us; then when we entered the neighborhood where the telephone office was, we had to hire another local guide for our guides. Then when we finally arrived at the telephone office, we hired another guide to open the door and lead us into the building. So in the span of about six blocks, we'd placed five guides on our payroll.

Walking past the colonial buildings in the main square on the first night, one could almost imagine the port in the days when orange peels were exported to France to make top-shelf Cointreau and Jacmel's coffee was enjoyed in European capitals. The haunting, soulful town was Haiti's major port in the 19th century—more important than Port-au-Prince. But that was all long ago.

Gone now from Jacmel is the sweet fragrance of orange peels drying in the sun on flat rooftops. Those citrus smells, according to those who remember, mixed with the pungent aroma of the coffee factory down on the waterfront to create a powerful, exotic aphrodisiac. Now, a rusted fishing boat has been abandoned in the middle of Jacmel's main waterfront street for more than a decade. Now, in Jacmel's soft breeze, you smell something less promising, more sinister. It's something you can't quite place: burning garbage? sweat? diesel exhaust? It is, perhaps, simply the smell of things falling apart.

Saíntil remembered that aphrodisiac, he told us, as we all lounged at a beachside bar and drank Haiti's excellent 15-year-old Barbancourt rum and watched garbage wash up in the surf. Years before, as a boy, he lived in one of sleepy rural villages near here, before he moved away to Port-au-Prince.

After Saíntil explained to us that his favorite actor was Shaquille O'Neal, we questioned him about his declaration about Papa Doc's mysticism from the morning. "Do you believe in voodoo?" we asked.

"No," he said resolutely, then thought for a moment: "I don't personally believe in voodoo. For myself. But I do believe that voodoo exists for many people."

Saíntil then switched topics to the national lottery and his method for picking the right numbers. Every night, Saíntil would try to dream of someone, and then play the number of letters in that person's name. "I dreamed a name last night that I have not dreamed of since childhood," Saíntil said. "Her name was Ghoslaine, and I loved her more than I ever loved anyone. I was so crazy in love, that if she had asked me to kill someone, I would have done it. I wanted her so bad."

"What happened?" we asked.

"She didn't love me back. But that was all long ago." Now, he said, he planned to play the number nine, for Ghoslaine, in the upcoming lottery.

Our 12-year-old guide reappeared in the bar and made another sales pitch for his "sister." Instead of accepting, we set them up at the bar and bought them both plates of chicken and rice, which they devoured.

At some point in the night, the bar ran out of rum, so Míchel wandered back to the room to get some of our own stash. When Míchel returned, he was visibly shaken. "Some kid on the beach just threatened me with a knife," he said. The bartender mixed us more rum-and-Cokes with our own rum. Then, without so much as a wink, charged us the full price.

*

The next day, Kevin and Míchel and I traveled along the red clay roads up to Cap-Rouge with Saíntil. Desir Guesler, one of IICA's technical advisors, joined us. We kicked up a thick dust that left a pinkish film on our truck and clothes.

Through several village markets, the hordes of people choked off the path; some poked their heads through our open windows and smiled. One ancient woman touched my face with her knotted hand and said simply, "Blanc." We continued along, and it took over an hour to travel just six kilometers. We passed wide cemeteries on the sides of the road, with massive tombs marking the dead.

Desir was a serious man who maintained an all-business face during the tour. "Before Haitian Bleu, the farmers didn't get a good price, so they clear-cut the trees and planted corn and beans," Desir said, pointing out patches of green vegetation on the primarily brown mountains. Farmers who grow Haitian Bleu, he showed us, are diversifying by planting a mix of coffee, cocoa, bananas, citrus, yams, and sugarcane.

We arrived at Cap-Rouge and saw the words ISIT NOU PWODUI BON KALITE KAFE—"Here we produce high quality coffee"— painted on the wall of the co-op's headquarters. This was where farmers for miles around brought their coffee beans for culling and sorting. Inside a dimly lit room, we were seated at a table with six farmers from the local co-op. We were told that ten thousand people from surrounding villages turned out when the president recently visited Cap-Rouge. "Our president ate right here at this table," said one of the men proudly, with Desir translating for us. "He promised to give us a secondary school."

"Also," Desir said. "Your vice president, Mr. Albert Gore, came right out of the sky in his helicopter and landed right here."

A woman appeared from the back room and poured coffee for everyone. The farmers watched with smiles on their faces as Kevin, Míchel, and I drank from tiny coffee cups. "It is not easy to process Haitian Bleu coffee," Desir told us. "It takes a lot of time. But it is worth it."

As he drank his coffee, Desir smiled for the first time. "Here is good people," he said. "In Port-au-Prince, there is no good people."

Later, the truck climbed higher up the mountain, to another co-op site in the village of Fond Jean Noel. We watched a man with a bag of coffee on his back making what would be a three-hour trip down the mountain. In Haiti, just to get the coffee off the mountain can be a great accomplishment.

When we arrived in Fond Jean Noel, a dozen half-naked children trailed us toward the cooperative, where we met Gesper, the cooperative's local vice president. Gesper showed us the storage room with dozens of bags of green coffee, the small cement yard where the beans are dried, and the pump-and-grind device used to remove the husks. "This pump was used by our president," Gesper boasted.

On our way back down the mountain, Kevin and Míchel requested another beer stop, and we sat on a cinderblock half-wall in a dirt-floored little café. Desir pointed out a huge white home across the street from the café, with a ten-foot gate, that belonged to an 80-year-old former Tontons Macoute. Dozens of people walked past and stared.

Saíntil looked extremely worried and rubbed his foot through his broken sandal. He apparently had cut it the day before, and now he wiped sweat off his brow and kept saying over and over that he feared he had a fever. Kevin, Míchel, and I could plainly see that what Saíntil had was a very infected toe and offered him some antibiotic ointment.

But Saíntil insisted it was something much more dire. When he was a baby, a voodoo priest told his parents that Saíntil would never in his life have a fever, like so many of the other sickly children in his village. The voodoo priest said he would only suffer one fever, late in life, as an older man. And this fever, the voodoo priest predicted, would be what finally killed Saíntil.

Saíntil reminded us that he was 49 years old. "That's not old," I said to console him. "Kevin and Míchel are almost that old." But what I knew from my research, and didn't say, was that the median life expectancy of a Haitian man was 47.1 years.

At breakfast on Carnival day, we watched a parade of children in costumes pass by our hotel's patio. Boys in purple tunics and fake swords danced in circles. Children with face paint and men with huge papier-mâché masks of dragons and lizards and spirits zigzagged down the road. A girl of about five, who seemed to be made of rubber, danced on a stick that was levitated by a half dozen teenage boys while an older man pounded on a drum. Three men who'd literally doused themselves with black motor oil and donned bull's masks, cracked long black whips in the middle of the street. After each performance, we placed gourdes in the dancers' outstretched hands.

Later, we walked to the beachside bar and watched a young boy breaking the antennae off live baby lobsters and tossing them into a basket. He would have been locked up in Maine for bringing in shellfish that tiny, but here it was only a matter of a few dollars, and he cooked us up some of the most tender lobster imaginable.

By this time, Kevin wore a straw hat painted fluorescent green and orange that he'd purchased right from the head of a Haitian man for a simple glass of rum. One of the whip-carrying boys covered in motor oil entered the bar and gyrated in the middle of the dance floor.

Our bartender, the same one who'd charged us for our own rum the night before, told us that cruise ships would soon be returning to Jacmel, calling here as they did thirty years ago. When we scoffed and pointed out all the garbage and metal debris littering the harbor, the bartender said with disdain, "Cruise ships already call at Cap Haitien in the north. The cruise companies just don't tell the Americans that they're coming to Haiti. They say it's a 'secret Caribbean island.'"

Saintil suggested we all go to a big cockfight that was happening on the outskirts of town and we agreed. As our truck approached the cockfight pit, more than two hundred eyes peered out from beneath a thatched roof. "Here comes the blanc money," said Míchel, under his breath, as we stepped out of the big white IICA truck.

A fight had already begun. Under the thatched roof, men cradled roosters, and each of the birds' heads was covered with a sock or a rag so their talons wouldn't be provoked. We bought a ticket and squeezed past bare-footed spectators who spilled off the wooden benches and leaned on one another to see two roosters tearing each other into a bloody mess. The fight took an agonizing twenty minutes, with the crowd cheering each time one of the cocks staggered backwards after a blow. Finally, one of them fell, and we watched money change hands.

Afterwards, in the sun, we watched a handler bring the losing rooster back to life by massaging it with a sponge. After kneading the poor, bloody, blinded animal for ten minutes, it finally began twitching again—perhaps to fight another day.

In the second fight, we decided to put our money on the rooster of a nice, toothless old man. The old man's son stood in the corner, sharpening the rooster's claws with a rusty knife. Each of us handed the bookie a hundred gourdes, and he scribbled something in pencil on a frayed sheet of paper.

What we soon learned about Haitian cockfighting was that arguing is nearly as important as the actual event. And so we waited, trying to decide if we wanted to continue to burn our skin in the sun or squeeze ourselves under the little thatched roof. We watched a woman ladling some type of red homemade liquor out of a huge washtub. Nearly a hundred men drank out of the same rusty metal cup. Míchel watched some others play a dice game on top of a makeshift table and figured out how the dealer teased the dice to his advantage. After Míchel won a dozen rolls in a row, the men changed the rules. After Míchel learned the new rules and won a few more rolls, the men told him he wasn't allowed to play anymore.

Finally, as the smell of a hundred bodies under a thatched roof reached its peak, the two cocks began fighting. But just as our rooster lunged for the other, our rooster's handler, the nice toothless old man, suddenly leaped into the ring and stood there screaming with outstretched hands. The whole pit soon erupted in Creole curses and yelling.

Saíntil translated the argument to us as if this sort of thing happened every day: The old man who jumped in the ring shouted that the opposing rooster was under a voodoo spell and that a zombie walked among the spectators at the cockfight. The old man declared that he was a powerful man and insisted upon standing in the ring to ward off the effects of the zombie. Of course, the other men under the thatched roof didn't like the idea of the old man standing in the middle of the cockfight and took issue.

Another half hour of arguing ensued, with a lot of shoving and pointing. Soon the fight was canceled. A young boy walked over and carefully counted bills and paid us back all of the money we'd bet. Judging from the tenor of the now-angry cockfight crowd, we decided to return to Jacmel before the next match started.

Later that evening, Kevin, Míchel, Saíntil and I lounged on the patio at our hotel with Barbancourt rum-and-Cokes and listened to a ragtag band consisting of ten men and only three instruments: a bongo, a homemade banjo, and a pair of maracas. The old man with the maracas, the band's leader, danced and sang haunting Creole ballads, though he had no front teeth. His white belt, cinched tight against his frail waist, looked as though it could never keep his baggy pants from falling down. Later, drunker, the bandleader would fall down, backwards, over his own wooden chair. "Donnez quel que chose pour la musique"—"Give something for the music," read a hand-drawn sign.

Kevin, who had visited Haiti on vacation with his wife back in the mid-1970s, requested a popular song he only half remembered. But when the band suddenly broke into the chorus—"Duvalier, Duvalier"—nearly half the bar cleared out. The only one still dancing was a prostitute in a dirty brown dress. A dozen boys who loitered in the street kept tapping us on the shoulder, over the patio railing, with their palms out, hoping for gourdes.

We returned to Port-au-Prince the same way we came. Along the way, we stopped at a place called Tombe Gateau, at the Haitian Bleu packinghouse, to meet with Stéphan Jean-Pierre. As we entered the dim, cinderblock packing house, we saw two dozen women sitting on the ground, each with a basket and a pile of green coffee beans, sorting the beans by size with their hands. These beans would soon be placed in burlap sacks and sent to roasters in the United States. Jean-Pierre said that, someday, Haitian Bleu would like to have its own roaster. "We want to have a roaster here by the time the cruise ships return to Jacmel," he said.

As Saíntil finally approached the outskirts of Port-au-Prince, he took a right turn up a gravel road and cruised through narrow streets bordered by shacks. He parked in front of a tiny blue house—his house. At least a dozen children with no shirts and shoes ran excitedly around the truck. Several of the older children stood with a basket of Chiclets, Chupa Chups lollipops, and cigarettes that they sold.

Saíntil brought us into his dark two-room house, introduced us to his wife, and showed us the ancient generator that gives his family four hours of electricity each night. At least two of these four hours are used to run a VCR that he proudly showed off. Saíntil cornered Kevin, showed him an oily, unidentifiable part from his circa-1960 generator, and asked if he would find a replacement when he returned to the United States.

Saíntil casually pointed out that his next-door neighbor was a voodoo priest. Above the house flew the telltale black, yellow, and red flag. We paid a visit to the voodoo priest and wandered through his temple. Murals of Christian saints, kings, and queens and bloody pictures of dragons and swords graced the walls, while in a corner sat bongos and the altar, crowded with dusty dark bottles, wooden staffs, and a tiny three-foot coffin. From the ceiling hung dozens of ripped plastic bags that read Carnation Evaporated Milk.

When we asked the priest if he could perform a ceremony for us, he refused. Then he said it would cost us several hundred dollars, and we refused. Saíntil explained that it would have been much too costly to prepare a voodoo feast for us, something he traditionally must do. The voodoo priest explained that this is why he rarely does ceremonies anymore.

Before we climbed back into the truck and continued on, Kevin, Míchel, and I unloaded our backpacks and gave away T-shirts, hats, pants, nearly everything to Saíntil's children. Once back on the road, Saíntil sighed and told us he'd dreamed once again of Ghoslaine. "Whatever happened to Ghoslaine?" I asked.

"When I was fifteen, I was so madly in love with Ghoslaine that I went to the voodoo priest in my village to make her fall in love with me," he said. The voodoo priest told Saíntil to bring him a brand-new handkerchief and a piece of candy and to pay him several gourdes, and the priest would cast a spell on Ghoslaine. "But I didn't have any money, and so for weeks I scoured the dirt below the coffee trees, for beans that the men had missed. And after many weeks, I had collected enough coffee to sell a sack and buy the candy and handkerchief and pay the priest."

So Saíntil returned to the priest, who took his money, ground up a love powder that he sprinkled on the candy and the handkerchief, and gave Saíntil these instructions: Have Ghoslaine accept the piece of candy from you and eat it; then tap her three times with the handkerchief; then express your undying love. "After that," Saíntil said, "the priest claimed she would be mine forever."

Saíntil did exactly as the priest instructed. Ghoslaine ate the candy, and he playfully tapped her three times with the handkerchief. And he told Ghoslaine that he loved her more than anyone else in the world. "Then I waited for a week, for two weeks, for a month for her to return my love. But after that day, she simply stopped coming around. I didn't know what to do. I went back to the voodoo priest, and he said that if I collected some more money, perhaps he could cast a more powerful spell."

But as Saíntil went back out into coffee fields to collect more coffee beans, he discovered that Ghoslaine had pledged her love to someone else—his best friend, a clever young man who'd taught himself English and wooed Ghoslaine in a way that the Creole-speaking Saíntil could never match.

"After that, I didn't believe in voodoo anymore," Saíntil said. "That's when I decided to run away from the country and move to Port-au-Prince. And more than everything else, I vowed to learn English." So Saíntil has been living in the squalor that is Port-au-Prince since the days of Duvalier. Though he once heard that she lives in France, Saíntil said he never saw or heard from the beautiful Ghoslaine ever again.

Saíntil's story stayed with me that night as we drank more rum and lost our money in the casino in Petionville. The story stayed with me as we flew away from Port-au-Prince the next day, and all I could see stretching out from the chaotic city was mile after mile of brown mountains baking treeless in the hot Caribbean sun. And since Saíntil's story is one about hope, and faith, and money, and love—and about the utter loss of all these things—his is the story that haunts me most when I think about my trip to Haiti. It haunts me whenever I see a particularly heartbreaking shade of brown. ✧

Extending Harry Crosby's "Brief Transit"

Edward Brunner

He had gifts that would have made him an explorer, a soldier of fortune, a revolutionist: they were qualities fatal to a poet.
—*Malcolm Cowley's summary of Harry Crosby*

Harry Crosby has been twice cursed with exceptional biographers (Malcolm Cowley in 1934 and Geoffrey Wolff in 1976) who were interested in exposing the sensational aspects of his too-brief existence—he died in 1929 at the age of 31 in a double-suicide pact that seemed made for tabloid headlines—but who were not particularly sympathetic to his writings. Those writings, to be sure, were not designed to be likable or even that accessible: avant-garde, experimental, surreal, emerging from a continental tradition that cultivated forms like the prose poem that were alien to Anglo-American modernism (though successfully explored by Williams). And Crosby did not become a compelling writer until the last years of his life. His apprenticeship, moreover, was particularly erratic, and worst of all, it unfolded in public, as Crosby's own press, Black Sun, released a steady stream of his work from 1927 onward.

Crosby no doubt first took up writing poetry much as he took up other amusements like living the expatriate life in France or owning racehorses or driving a Bugatti. His independent wealth, multiplied as a result of the favorable exchange rate enjoyed by the American dollar in post-war Europe, allowed him such indulgences as refurbishing a medieval mill for living quarters outside Paris or taking extended traveling tours, or experimenting with photography, or learning to fly solo in an aeroplane, a gadget still so new in 1929 that no one had agreed on its spelling. But it is too simple to portray Crosby as a fugitive from a bad Scott Fitzgerald novel, though that was exactly the way Malcolm Cowley notoriously introduced him in *Exile's Return* (1934), in which the trajectory of his life, from excess to doom, came to represent the ups and downs of the Roaring Twenties. Geoffrey Wolff broke from Cowley's example by refusing to accord Crosby representative status, but his decision instead to focus on Crosby as exemplifying a weak and indulgent character, while it made for a gripping (if heavily moralistic) narrative, hardly served to promote interest in his writings.

Crosby's beginnings suggest how easily a legend could grow up around him. His family was old-line Boston and wealthy: his Uncle Jack, who opened doors for young Harry in the banking industry, was J. P. Morgan. Yet Crosby never fit into the type of the spoiled aristocrat. After graduating from the exclusive boy's prep school St. Mark's in 1917, he promptly volunteered for the American Field Service Ambulance Corps. He became part of a New England tradition whereby sons of the elite, from Robert Gould Shaw and Thomas Wentworth Higginson in the Civil War to E. E. Cummings in World War I, carved out a special role for themselves in a conflict that they could easily have avoided. In France, he was at the Battle of Somme, and when America officially entered the War, he enlisted with the U. S. Army Ambulance Corps and served at the Second Battle of Verdun. After the Battle of Orme, his section (the 29th, attached to the 120th French Division) was cited for bravery, and in 1919 Crosby was awarded the *Croix de Guerre.*

Crosby's return to Boston to attend Harvard under an accelerated program for veterans led to his graduation in 1921. He had met, in the meantime, his future wife—then with the name of "Polly" ("Caresse" was a later invention), and six years older than he, married to another and with two young children. Their courtship was tempestuous—it scandalized blue-blood Boston—and when they were at last married, in a dramatic ceremony in New York City, his family was perhaps relieved to think of the couple taking up residence in far-off Paris, where he had previously been employed in a branch of one of Uncle Jack's many banks. Certainly Crosby expressed relief at returning to Paris and residing among other young expatriates, on the fringes of the bohemian left bank, with artists and writers mingling among the wealthy.

Settling in France, the Crosbys traveled in Europe, purchased first one race horse then two more, visited North Africa (where they first sampled opium, an indulgence to which they would return over the years), and visited Spain. From 1922 to 1925, the Crosbys led a life not untypical of the comfortably well-off expatriate. This began to change in 1925 when Crosby arranged dual publication of books of poetry by his wife and by him. (Around the same time, his wife became "Caresse.") When Crosby's *Sonnets for Caresse* arrived on the desk of Harriet Monroe in *Poetry*, she reviewed it favorably. In April 1927, the Crosbys officially launched the Black Sun Press. Along with fine art versions by classic writers (like Poe) in the kind of deluxe illustrated editions that were favored by wealthy collectors, the new press also published Crosby's second collection, *Red Skeletons,* poetry heavily indebted to Baudelaire and the turn-of-the-century British "decadent" tradition exemplified by Oscar Wilde and Arthur Symons. In October 1927, Crosby inherited the bulk of famous expatriate (and close friend of Edith Wharton) Walter Berry's library (Berry was a cousin, and he and Harry had visited in Europe since 1923). Crosby's affection for books and for libraries was evident in the delight with which he received Berry's 7,000-volume library, but it is also present in two unpublished essays from this period in which he so lovingly described the look and feel of well-printed volumes he had rescued from bookstalls that he eroticized the experience: "I would rather inhale the smell of ruin in *The Punishments of China*, its ecclesiastical odor of charred incense, its aroma of dead leaves and long-abandoned castle halls, than smell the contents of a cobwebbed bottle of Napoleon brandy, or gunpowder along the road to Bras."

While Crosby continued to maintain a glamorous and luxurious lifestyle that included an "open marriage" and that was financed by selling the bonds and stocks whose dividends were the basis of his income, he also began to read deeply in contemporary literature. Since the important artists who were painting, writing and performing in Paris occupied a demimonde that often intersected with the wealthy and the bored, Crosby's amusements in effect constituted a hands-on education in the tenets of experimental modernism. He shook off the influences of the decadents, recognizing how out-of-date his education had been. He started to sell off hundreds of the volumes that he had inherited from Berry as he cultivated a taste for current writing. As part of his new self-education, he became fascinated by versions of suicide, drawn especially toward narratives of artists who killed themselves. He developed an obsessive interest in imagery that was centered on the sun, and he found that by returning to such imagery in his own writing he would always have a ready supply of material. The "black sun" has been described as a concept intended to unite powerful forces of life and death—an effort to unify conflicting archetypes—but as a visual design, it no doubt had sexual significance. Every doodle of a "black sun" that Crosby added to his signature also includes an arrow, jutting upward from the "y" in Crosby's last name and aiming toward the center of the sun's circle: a phallic thrust received by a welcoming erogenous zone.

Through the end of 1927, Crosby began viewing his own writing practice with a new self-consciousness. Most important was his decision to reconstruct and produce a diary that was both a chronicle of the times and an expressive, innovative work of art. The final concept of this diary only emerged after proceeding through several stages. Crosby had always kept diaries and working notebooks, but the idea of combining them into something publishable began when he worked that summer of 1927 to prepare a lengthy typescript entitled "Shadow of the Sun" whose exact nature eludes description. Its numbered passages (over 230 in all, and 110 manuscript pages long) are remarkably diverse. One passage offers a compressed description of an event while another records a quote discovered while reading; some passages are brief four- or five- word phrases, while others may be lengthy lists of favorite words; still others convey in terse, imagistic detail, his impressions of a trip to North Africa. This particular text, however, Crosby never published. Having originated in rough diary-like notes, it was now returned to that form, but in a thoroughly reconstructed manner, in a "diary" that presented itself as covering daily events from 1922 to 1926. The sets of numbered paragraphs were now reshaped and expanded into a sequence of dated diary entries. Almost all of the passages were rewritten to provide more informative detail. Several of the original 230 passages were set aside, to be collected later as the prose poems in *Torchbearer* (Crosby's final published volume, printed posthumously, although it mostly included work from this initial stage in his development). At the same time, other writings that he had previously composed as individual poems or prose poems were now folded back into the reconstructed diary, as if they were observations that had simply occurred on a certain day. Out of this thorough reshaping emerged a "diary" of the years 1922-1926, which Crosby entitled *Shadows of the Sun,* first in a series of three that would be published by the Black Sun Press.

Crosby began to take action to live up to his new role as a diarist. In 1928, he became a regular contributor to Eugene Jolas's *transition*, eventually offering financial support and serving as an advisory editor. The Black Sun Press published fiction by D. H. Lawrence, poetry by Archibald MacLeish, and more poetry by Caresse, as well as two new collections of Crosby's poetry, *Chariot of the Sun* and *Transit of Venus.* In one sense, *Chariot of the Sun* was an outrageous and indulgent collection—almost a dada stunt. The sun commands the major role in every work. It has become an inescapable presence, powerful, vivid, but also obsessive, even menacing. In another sense, though, the collection is a marvel, one man's exhibit of the discursive options open to the neophyte modernist poet at this distinct moment in literary history. Crosby's voracious appetites also included extensive reading, and Chariot of the Sun is a virtuoso demonstration, a set of textbook-perfect examples that include variations on the sonnet, *vers libre*, the five-line "cinquaine" poem developed by Adelaide Crapsey, descriptive travelogues in the tradition of the French prose poem, poems composed entirely of lists (some of which are devotedly encyclopedic, others of which ridicule the idea of making a list), understated love poems that echo T. S. Eliot at his most dryly delicate (one begins: "Young Raymonde in her robe de style / Is far more beautiful / Than Venus Anadyomene / Or naiad in a pool"), and what D. H. Lawrence would name as a "sound poem"—a string of apparent nonsense syllables (its first line reads: "Sththe fous on ssu cod") that were, in fact, a personal cipher that could be decoded as "harry poet of the sun."

If *Chariot of the Sun* was deliberately staged, *Transit to Venus* was a more intimate work, an up-to-date version of the sonnet sequence that

Crosby had once produced for Caresse but which was now inspired by a disturbingly passionate affair with Josephine Rotch, one of the many beautiful young women with whom he would be intimately involved. (Though Crosby's marriage could be described as a series of affairs, only Josephine inspired her own complete book.) Familiar declarations of passion are here filtered through a nontraditional idiom, as in "Lost Things." If the lover addressed in Sonnets to Caresse was on familiar terms with Baudelaire's work, the lover addressed in Transit to Venus is fashionably aware of Gertrude Stein.

Lost things
Were warm with beauty
Birds of the
Birds of the have nests
Her charming gestures and her breasts
Hurtle in the darkened room,
So soft, so hushed
So soft the birds in nests,
So soft her breasts.

Toward the end of 1928, the Crosbys returned to America for visits of several weeks in Boston and New York. Crosby's deepening engagement with his own writing is evident in the notebooks he kept during this visit—notebooks packed with overheard dialogue, with examples of advertising, with fragments of new poems, all of which he mined over the next few months, when he had returned to France. Coming to the urbanized American east after his long stay in Europe, and at a time when the whole pace of American life was increasing, Crosby was astonished by a life style that seemed to be more excessive than anything he had dreamed of. In a visit two years earlier, in 1926, before Crosby saw himself as a modernist poet, he had been distressed by an America that he was quick to condemn for its ugliness, for its un-European bustle. In a prose poem from this 1926 visit, he looked out from the observation deck of an express speeding down the Shore Line from Boston to New York and described the surrounding billboards as pouring forth a verbiage—"four out of five will get pyorrhea brush your teeth with Fordham's for the gums more than a toothpaste it checks pyorrhea" —that was no more meaningful than the "clickety-click clickety-click" of rail joints with which he began this particular prose poem. "Industrialism is triumphant," he pronounces, "as ugliness, sordid ugliness is everywhere destroying beauty ..."

In 1928, however, he found himself, as he wrote to his parents, "pro-America" or at least pro–New York City. He was both elated and appalled by the vulgarity of a business culture that advertised by day and night, that dominated the cityscape and lit up the evening sky as if it had no need of the sun (it carried its own suns with it). His writings are newly galvanized by these contradictory feelings, and his notebooks are filled with sketches and fragments that portray New York City as a dark paradise of commercialization. Now in 1928 when he looks out from the observation car of the Merchant's Express he experiences something like visual splendor and a particularly modern music:

> we sit outside on the observation car and listen to the clickety-click clickety-clack clickety click click click and the rattling over the switches clickety click click click clack (Symphony of the Rails—there is no other Symphony) and we watch the red and green signal lights and the great electrical signs (Nujol for Constipation) and the gold windows of the buildings and the blaze of light from the streets below.

Elsewhere, in drafts and fragments recorded in a notebook, the American propensity for making rules and listing prohibitions catches his eye. In phrases that list actual warnings ("sitting or lying on flowerbeds or other beds is forbidden"), Crosby evokes dangers both real and imagined, suggesting a Puritan obsession with sexuality that in itself erotically charges the atmosphere.

Returning to France at the beginning of 1929, Crosby continued to meet poets and writers, including Hart Crane (with whom he arranged to publish The Bridge in a deluxe edition) and D. H. Lawrence. Other Black Sun Press projects included works by James Joyce and Kay Boyle, and a volume of photography by Gretchen and Pete Powel. He organized and published a new collection entitled *Mad Queen*, in which he experimented with parataxis as an organizing principle. The linguistic becomes a new interest. Now writings can revolve self-reflexively around sets of words that Crosby endlessly tests in varying situations that twist, erase, mock, and sometimes even (though rarely) elevate them. "Mad" and "madness" are first among this new vocabulary. In works that appeared in *transition*, he testified to the new influence of James Joyce, then immersed in Finnegans Wake). In one of a series of prose poems entitled "A Short Introduction to the Word," he coined words that were both outrageous yet appropriate to a new age: "Auroramor, Barbarifire, Parabolaw, Lovegown, Nombrilomane."

Crosby also ventured into other artistic areas. He had used photography earlier in his life to record his World War I experiences. Those war photos were carefully mounted in one of the dozen scrapbooks that Harry and Caresse maintained together—elaborate productions that included press clippings, possible topics for poetry, society-page news, memorabilia and ephemera (hotel bills, racing club membership cards, Christmas greetings), appealing magazine covers, and photographs of all kinds, from family snapshots to provocative nudes. But the photography that began to hold his interest in 1929 was serious work, in line with the material that Jolas, with his sharp eye for the current and the controversial, had been including in *transition*. Francis Brugiere, Charles Sheeler, Lazlo Moholy-Nagy, El Lissitzky, Eugene Atget, Tina Modotti, Berenice Abbott, and Man Ray all had photos reproduced in transition in just the two years that Crosby was associated with the journal. Photography in the 1920s was fighting to declare itself an equal among the visual arts by offering images that were both recognizable and abstract. Crosby used his camera's frame-making powers not to distort objects—all remain identifiable—but to tease unexpected associations from their lines and their structure. Some images explore the interplay between the fragility of the human body and the fragility of the airplane—in 1929, a contraption that looked homemade and piecemeal. In other photos, powerful cranes that construct massive buildings are made to look as delicate as birds. Railroad right of way signals resemble alien creatures. Smokestacks and funnels take on the shapes of intriguing sculpture. In still other photos, Crosby aimed the camera at his own body and the bodies of others, at the displays for shoppers in windows, at race track crowds, and at an inflatable toy horse (disarmingly posed in a number of settings, often as if it were a much-loved infant).

Crosby also began taking flight lessons in 1929, and he completed his first solo flight on November 11, Armistice Day, eleven years after the end of World War I (an event he noted in his notebooks and carried over into his diaries). He signaled his new mastery of the air by completing *Aphrodite in Flight*, a seventy-five paragraph how-to manual for lovers that explores the similarities between flying planes and making love to a woman. Parodically invoking the cool crisp prose of an eighteenth century French book of aphorisms, the paragraphs sometimes read like a dadaist gimmick, sometimes like sophisticated and cynical advice: "For long flights there must be a sufficient reserve of gasoline, for long love affairs a sufficient reserve of gold." Much less emotionally detached was a second sequence of prose poems from 1929 entitled *Sleeping Together*. In a notebook he jotted: "Transit of Venus (for Josephine) / Sleeping Together (for Caresse)/ (these are the two books I have written which are damn good the others can go to hell)." First presented in excerpts in *transition* as transcripts of actual dreams, these prose poems became, when rewritten to include a "you" who also figures centrally within them, a testament to a deeply erotic and playful relationship that he associated, through particular textual details, with Caresse:

The Ritz Tower sways like a drunkard under the cold fire of the moon while you sit in your lace pyjamas at the edge of the bed busily cutting your toe nails to the great astonishment of a bottle of gin which stares out at you from behind a pair of my white tennis shoes.

He painstakingly copied out a longhand text as a gift to her on his arrival in New York City in December 1929.

The sensational suicide that occurred on December 10 caught his friends by surprise. In the company of Josephine Rotch (now a newly married Josephine Bigelow), the same who had inspired the writing of *Transit to Venus*, he was found with a .25 caliber gunshot wound in his right temple (she was fatally wounded in the left). They had been together for much of the last week, following an elaborate itinerary that she had insisted they follow and that had taken them, among other places, to several days in a hotel in Detroit. On the day before their death, Josephine had delivered a passionate letter that, in its chant-like listing of the characteristics that they held in common, eerily resembled one of Crosby's own poems. The 35-line missive, divided into seven stanzas and entitled *There are things I know* and dedicated "For Harry," ends by insisting

that the sun is *our* God
and that death is *our* marriage

Josephine died first, the coroner concluded; then some hours later, Crosby killed himself—possibly filling the time in between with entries in his notebook. These important last pages of his notebook are difficult to identify with certainty. When they were edited posthumously by Caresse, pages were shuffled, and passages were culled out as if they were likely candidates for being reshaped into diary entries, had Harry lived.

Crosby had been talking about death for the last five years, ever since he had compiled a notebook in French of quotations from literary figures, philosophers and essayists who upheld the idea of suicide. He had even set a date for the time that he and Caresse would fly together into the sun in their own white airplane. But that date was 1942, eleven years in the future, and the description was more like a passage from one of his surrealist prose poems than anything contractual. To Crosby's suicide, Hart Crane reacted with disbelief and then disgust, describing it as another "experiment" that Crosby had decided to undertake; Crane said he was reserving his grief for Caresse, the one who was the true victim. Gretchen Powel, among those who knew him intimately, flatly refused to believe he had set out to kill himself. Just three days earlier, he had taken the fragments jotted down in his working notebook and, as he had done regularly for several years, reshaped them into versions of the diary entries that he had been publishing in the series entitled *Shadows of the Sun*. (It is true, these particular reshapings were unusually terse.) His notebooks were filled with plans for new poetry, including several sequences, and a dozen pieces published in *transition* awaited collection; numerous Black Sun projects were underway; and several dozen recent photographs (including a shipboard sequence that may have been taken on this trip to New York) had been developed in small contact-sheet sizes, with their images ready to be enlarged. Events of the moment had somehow overwhelmed all these plans for the future.

After his death, Caresse carried on the publication of the Black Sun Press, completing a sumptuous edition of *The Bridge*, with three photographs that were the debut of Walker Evans, and releasing a "collected Crosby"—four books that reprinted earlier collections. One of these collections had been originally introduced by D. H. Lawrence. To accompany it, Caresse solicited essays for the other three from T. S. Eliot, Ezra Pound, and Stuart Gilbert. Caresse went on, then, to continue the tradition of fine publication, culminating in the release, in the late 1940s, of several issues of Portfolio, a remarkable collection of both American and English writers, with several contributions by Europeans in translation that also featured prints by artists both novice and well-known. Photos by Harry, along with a selection of some of his poems, appeared in three issues.

What Caresse did not do, however, was attempt to assemble from Harry's finished typescripts, publications in *transition*, and holograph manuscripts a representative collection of work from his final years. It no doubt would have been emotionally difficult for her to do so. His letters and his diaries only emphasized just how strong his attachment had been to the woman with whom he had been when he killed himself. And judging by Caresse's own poetry, which generally avoided the extremes that Harry had embraced, she would have been hesitant to freely endorse the aesthetics of much of his later work. The volumes she produced as a homage to him were limited to those that he himself had organized and already published, including *Torchbearer*, a selection of early prose poetry that he had assembled in the winter of 1929 and *Aphrodite in Flight*. But his larger projects were never reconstructed, and no effort was made to bring together the work he had published but left uncollected. The "collected " Crosby that Caresse put forward inadvertently downplayed his later work.

Crosby, to be sure, remains a figure of enigmatic proportions. Unlike other writers who died at too early an age, he left behind him no commanding set of works that represent an unconditional achievement. He was, it would appear, still in process. But his work is not what it has been accused of being: "Outsider Art," the confused product of a mind unhinged by excess. Crosby brings to a continental tradition of experiment an eye that is particularly fresh and bright. His responses to the booming business culture of New York and Boston are more than just satirical dismissals: he is both offended and enraptured by display on such a scale. And perhaps because he actually had the means to afford swift cars and to learn to fly a plane, he was in a position to experience the speed of a new era (he was genuinely surprised when Hart Crane, a heretofore fearless companion in almost any adventure, blanched at the idea of hopping on a plane for a quick trip to England). And in all his work there is a strong imprint of the erotic. Crosby's confidence in himself – which might seem narcissistic, or worse, the annoying self-absorption of the very wealthy – is unshakable, but it is inseparable from a pervasive sexuality that has positive associations with freedom.

Less than a handful of critics ever thought to challenge the prevailing view of Crosby as a poetic failure. Sy Kahn assembled a selected poems in 1977 and linked Crosby with the visionary aesthetics of Hart Crane; Victor Reed in 1969 decoded the text from Chariot of the Sun that had been previously thought to be nonsense (and analyzed by D. H. Lawrence as such). Cary Nelson, in *Repression and Recovery* (1989), was first to remark upon Crosby's diversity and to suggest an approach to reading his work. A pamphlet that selected wisely from Crosby's work was privately printed in 1995 by Sara Sowers and Greg Newsome. And at the moment, a broad selection of Crosby's uncollected writings is available on the Modern American Poetry Site (MAPS), designed to accompany the *Oxford Anthology of Modern American Poetry*, edited by Cary Nelson. Displayed at www.english.uiuc.edu/maps/poets/a_f/crosby/crosby.htm, these excerpts (drawn from material catalogued and maintained under the direction of David Koch, Shelley Cox, and Katharine Salzmann of Special Collections in the Morris Library of Southern Illinois University at Carbondale) offer a view of this poet that will be enlarged further in a forthcoming edition of Crosby's poems, prose poems and photographs in the American Recovery Series published by the University of Illinois Press. ❖

NOON

1369 MADISON AVENUE   PMB 298   NEW YORK   NEW YORK   10128-0711

SUBSCRIPTION $9 DOMESTIC AND $14 FOREIGN